LEGEND, MYTH and HISTORY in the OLD TESTAMENT

LEGEND, MYTH and HISTORY in the OLD TESTAMENT

by

WARREN W. JACKSON
ST. PAUL'S SCHOOL
Concord, N.H.

with an introduction by

HARVEY H. GUTHRIE, Jr.
Dean of The Episcopal Theological School
Cambridge, Mass.

Independent School Press

Wellesley Hills Massachusetts

PRINTED IN THE UNITED STATES OF AMERICA

0-88334-031-3

CONTENTS

FOREWORD

Textbooks come about in many ways. *Legend, Myth and History in the Old Testament* was written because of the need for a secondary school text on the Old Testament and the history of Israel that would reflect modern biblical-historical scholarship on a sophisticated, but relatively uncomplicated level. The book grew out of an actual classroom situation at St. Paul's School, where the Rev. Warren Jackson was teaching.

This particular class is a joint venture involving the Sacred Studies and History Departments of the School, and is team-taught by the men of both disciplines. Simultaneously, the need for texts was felt by both departments and so Mr. Jackson produced *Legend and Myth,* and Mr. Kellogg, of the History Department, wrote *Out of the Past.* The latter (also published by the Independent School Press) is a history of the ancient near eastern and classical worlds. The two books are complementary in that they are products of the day-to-day experience of the same class; but they are different in approach and method, which has proved to be a valuable learning experience in itself. Thus, the books can be used together or separately. We at St. Paul's have found using the books together and team-teaching the course on a full-year basis to be an extremely stimulating experience, both for the students and for the teachers.

Legend and Myth was a daily production. This is true in a very literal sense in that the author produced each chapter for immediate classroom use. Sections were mimeographed and distributed to the students as they were completed. Mr. Jackson intended to revise the book at a later date, but his death occurred before he could complete that task. The Sacred Studies Department has continued to use the book in its rough form, but we have been convinced of the desirability of publication, not only for our own use, but also for other secondary schools.

Publication necessitated editing, which presented problems. How much can be changed in a work without the author's consent, before it is no longer solely his work? With that in mind, the editing has been as limited as possible, dealing primarily with grammatical and textual errors. In one or two places, where the MS was incomplete, it was necessary to second guess Mr. Jackson. This was done sparingly and only after consulting his lecture notes. Consequently, the writer of this Forward claims only to be an editor and not a revisor; the book, as it stands, is the work of Warren Jackson.

The book is not meant to be read alone, but in conjunction with the original biblical material. The use of the Oxford Annotated edition of the *Revised Standard Version of the Bible* is recommended because this is the edition most frequently used in the textbook and the students have found the footnotes and introductions helpful.

A special thanks should be made to Mr. Philip Burnham of the English Department at St. Paul's for his suggestions and help in correcting the grammatical errors.

St. Paul's School
June, 1970

Driss Knickerbocker

INTRODUCTION

Introducing the Old Testament to modern readers and students is no easy task. In the Old Testament we are not only dealing with a book that is not really one book, but a book that comes from the life and history of Israel stretching over some eight or ten centuries. Not only does the book as a whole have a complex history, but with rare exceptions each separate book within the Old Testament has a complex history if its own. Furthermore, this complexity requires more than skill in literary analysis, more than dexterity at separating out various sources and strands and strata, more than sensitivity to varying genre and literary forms. It requires the ability to use the results of archaeological and historical research in such a way as to relate the material in the Old Testament to the history and the culture which was its setting. That is true not only in the obvious sense, but because the Old Testament itself takes history and culture to be of theological significance.

But there is more to it than that. What the Old Testament has to say is said in language and forms and concepts that are separated from the modern, Western student not only by thousands of years but by vast cultural and linguistic differences. The interpreter, if he is to do an adequate job, must deal with the principles of interpretation. He must give attention to the *nature* of the materials with which he is dealing as compared with the nature of modern literary materials. Specifically, he must devote attention to the characteristics of and the problems raised by the kind of narrative we now classify as myth or legend, to Hebrew anthropology as compared with modern views of the nature of man, to the Hebrew conception of God in contrast to more philosophical theologies.

Moreover, if the modern interpreter of the Old Testament is writing to provide the basis of an introduction of that book to students in courses in schools, he must arrange his material in such a way that it is clear, that it fits into the realities of class hours and assignments, that it can be handled within the framework available.

It seems to me that Warren Jackson has, in this book, succeeded on all counts. He begins by examining modern views of the Bible so that the prejudices and presuppositions of the readers are taken into account. He does not treat the narratives of a book like Genesis without first going into the question of the nature of those narratives. He relates the historical books to the historical and social and political situations of the times from which they come and to which they refer. He constantly pauses to deal with theological and anthropological concepts that must be understood if the Old Testament writings themselves are to be understood. His treatment of the Old Testament is chronological so that the various books and parts of books are seen in a perspective compatible to modern ways of thinking. And his material is arranged in such a way as to make it usable in the situation of the school and classroom.

I would like, as an Old Testament scholar and teacher myself, to commend two things in particular about this book. The first is that the author is obviously competent in the sense that he knows not only the biblical material, but that he is thoroughly acquainted with the critical issues that have emerged through centuries of Old Testament study. He writes clearly and lucidly, with the sure hand of a teacher skilled in the presentation of his material. But behind what he writes the scholar in the field recognizes sure knowledge of all that is involved. The second thing is that the author does not, given his competence in the field, present a mere catalogue of all the interpretations given in the boring kind of way that so often "turns off" real interest in the subject. Having weighed the issues and the different positions taken, he is not afraid to take a position himself (even some with which I do not agree!). This is true, for example, of his interpretation of the sacred Ark of Israel, and of the way in which he sets down the prophecies of Amos separating out primary and secondary material. The reader should know that not every expert would agree with every conclusion reached or implied on these pages. That I take to be a virtue. It makes for an interesting rather than a dull book. It makes for a book in which the author takes the reader into his own thinking, into the excitement of conclusions reached after real study. For those who will respond, it opens up the process of discovery that is what scholarship and education are all about.

So, I salute this book, and commend it. And I cannot finish without paying tribute to the author as well as the book. I am honored to have been asked to write this foreword, both as the Dean of the theological school from which Warren Jackson was graduated and as the father of a student who worked with the material of this book in earlier form. After being trained as a naval architect and pursuing a career in the Navy and as a civilian in naval architecture and nuclear engineering, Warren Jackson entered the Episcopal Theological School to graduate and be ordained at the age of thirty-seven. He then spent nine years as a teacher in the Sacred Studies department of St. Paul's School. His untimely death in 1967 robbed the church and education of a man respected for his competence, his integrity, and his spirit. I am deeply thankful for the opportunity to commend LEGEND, MYTH AND HISTORY IN THE OLD TESTAMENT not only as a valuable and useful treatment of the Hebrew scriptures, but as a treasured heritage from his life and work.

Harvey H. Guthrie, Jr.

LEGEND, MYTH and HISTORY in the OLD TESTAMENT

Chapter I

LITERALISM AND FUNDAMENTALISM

A. Literalism

Literalism is the acceptance of written or spoken material as though it were an accurate physical description of the event with which it is concerned. Its content and meaning depend upon and are faithful to *the letter* (litera). In a similar sense obedience to "the letter of the law" is an unimaginative and exact conformity to a written or spoken code of behavior. Literalists assume that there is an exact correspondence between the written or spoken word, forever fixed in writing or in the collective memory of man, and some physical event, forever frozen in time past.

As a simple example of literalism consider the beginning of a typical day for a modern man. The possibility of sleep is removed by the persistence of a radio alarm clock. Reluctantly he struggles back to consciousness against a background of news reports, weather forecasts, and a commercial diatribe extolling the virtues of beer and cigarettes. Gradually the world comes into focus. The exaggerated and distorted fears, the irrational dreams and unsound decisions of the night gradually disappear. The hard, sharp world of reality becomes a fact.

An account of this event as written by a literalist would read as follows:

> At 6:25 a.m. the radio-alarm went off. After listening to the news, the weather, and some commercials, Mr. X. arose, dressed, and set out to meet the new day.

This "factual account" has not said anything untrue. It has failed, however, to convey anything about the significance of the event. It says nothing of the grinding monotony of an ordered existence, of convictions about the purpose of life which drive a man to contend with it day after day or of the morality involved in modern advertising.

Another problem that faces the literalist is the fact that many descriptions of stories were never intended to be taken literally. Some discrimination must be used in deciding what material should be so classified, and then establishing how it was meant to be interpreted. Even the most innocent child realizes that Aesop was not primarily recording a talking fox's observation about the sourness of grapes. When it becomes necessary to decide which parts of the Bible ought to be taken literally the problem suddenly becomes much more complex.

B. Fundamentalism

Fundamentalism is a position which holds that the total content of the Bible is to be interpreted literally. This position leads to such beliefs as a conviction that all things were created by God in six days some 4000 years ago, that the first man and woman were Adam and Eve, and that Jonah was swallowed by a large fish. The fundamentalist view has been held by many people for various reasons. The principal ones are these:

1. Fundamentalism has the advantage of simplicity. No decision has to be made concerning which of several possible ways the numerous parts of the Bible ought to be interpreted.
2. By assuming that the Bible is sacred and inspired it is held in awe. There is a hesitancy to tamper with it by reading meanings into it. The safest course is to accept it literally.
3. There is no need to come to grips with difficult material such as descriptions of miraculous events, direct contradictions (such as the order of creation in Genesis 1 and 2), unseemly conduct such as the drunkenness of Noah. A

literal acceptance of the content plus an assumption of uniform sanctity for all of it, makes interpretation superfluous.

In this course we shall examine the contents of the Old Testament from the assumption that not all of it was written to be interpreted literally. Part of our task will be to separate the material in preparation for its interpretation. This is necessary because the contents of the Bible were written by different people, in different times and places, for different reasons. We shall begin with the study of Genesis and with the assumption that the content of this book can be most conveniently classified into two categories, namely legend and myth.

C. Legend and Myth

When any literary material is classified as a legend or a myth there is usually an unconscious reaction which brands these writings as worthless as far as historical value goes. If anything, it is either tolerated as being quaintly amusing or it is condemned as being totally impractical. None of these viewpoints are correct. There are many clues concerning historical origins of races in both legends and myths. The philosophical, religious, and moral content of such writings is often profound.

We shall use the words *legend and myth* in a precise and particular way. The following definitions will hold throughout our study of the Bible.

> A myth is a story the main purpose of which is to convey a fundamental moral truth. Its content may or may not be based upon an historical event.
>
> A legend is a story the main purpose of which is to describe the origins of a tribe or race. Its content is based at least in part upon historical events.

The book of Genesis is composed of five myths and four legends. They are as follows:

Myths

1. The Creation

2. Adam and Eve
3. Cain and Abel
4. Noah and the Ark
5. The Tower of Babel

Legends
1. Abraham
2. Isaac
3. Jacob
4. Joseph

Before examining the content of Genesis in detail it is first necessary to examine its literary origins – who wrote it, when, and where.

CHAPTER II

THE AUTHORS OF GENESIS

A. The Old Agreement and the New

Even though the immediate object of our study is the book of Genesis, the primary necessity is to consider the authorship of the first five books of the Bible, namely, Genesis, Exodus, Leviticus, Numbers, and Deuteronomy. Taken together, these books are called the Pentateuch. They are referred to as *The Books of Moses* because they concern themselves with the Law, and Moses was the chief law-giver.[1] The Law is summarized in the Ten Commandents. It embodies every aspect of the relationship between God and the Hebrews. Although the Law and its many details may seem dead and sterile to us, for the Hebrews it was a way of life. The relationship which the Law governed was a covenant or agreement between God and the descendents of Abraham. If they worship him only and obey his commandments, they will prosper and endure as a nation. If they break the agreement, the inevitable consequences are war, destruction, desolation, and ruin. This is the old agreement or the old covenant or the Old Testament. It stands in contrast to the new agreement[2] between God and all men. In essence the new agreement promises eternal life to those who accept Jesus as Lord. The new agreement became necessary when man proved himself unable to keep the terms of the Mosaic Law.

B. The Pentateuch

The first five books of the Bible form a unit in that they summarize the basic Hebrew belief that God is the creator and sustainer of the universe. They support the thesis that he has revealed himself and his purpose in a unique way within the history of the Hebrews and through the terms of the covenant. These Books were written by several authors in various times and places. They were combined into their present form by many editors.

In spite of these complicated origins, four distinct and basic written sources are distinguishable. These written sources are in turn based upon oral tradition which is now lost. Oral tradition is not unique to the Hebrews. It forms the basis of the historical records of every ancient race.

Since the names of the authors (or in some cases schools of authorship) of the Pentateuch are not known, each distinguishable section has been assigned an authorship which is designated by a letter. The letters are J, E, D, and P. These sections are attributable to different writers because they vary in style, content, grammatical structure, point of view, interest, and historical data.

C. J, E, D, and P

1. J. The earliest author of the Pentateuch is called J. His date is c. 850 B. C. He is called J because he refers to God as Yahweh or Jahweh. J's interest often lies in events in southern Palestine; therefore it is assumed that he is a native of Judah. His style is simple and direct. It is easy to read. His view of God is anthropomorphic, that is, he thinks of God in human terms. He describes God as walking in the Garden of Eden in the cool of the day, and has him closing the door of the ark for Noah.

2. E. Chronologically, E is the next author. His date is c. 750 B. C. He is called E because he refers to God as Elohim. His interest is in the prophetic activities in northern Palestine[3] and so he is assumed to be a native of Ephraim. His view of God is slightly less anthropomorphic than J's. God is a bit further removed and slightly more aloof. E's style is somewhat more formal than J's.

3. D. D is the name given to the school of authors

responsible for the Book of Deuteronomy. Their date is 621 B. C. Their interest is in the Law and the style of writing is legalistic and formal.

4. P. P represents a school of authorship known as the Priestly School. The date is c. 450 B. C. Writings of the Priestly School show a dry, dull, repetitive style. The interest of this School is almost exclusively with the priesthood and the Law, and with the details of worship and sacrifice in the Temple.

We are now ready to turn our attention to the contents of Book of Genesis. It was written by three authors: J, E and P. It contains two kinds of stories, legends and myths.

[1]It should be understood that Moses did not write these books. His name was associated with them even from earliest times in order to enhance their status as a law to be obeyed.

[2]Which is the subject of the New Testament.

[3]E may be associated with the prophetic activity of Elijah and Elisha.

Chapter III

THE CREATION MYTH

A. The Hebrew World View

In considering the five myths in Genesis it is essential to keep our definition of myth constantly in mind. A myth is a story the main purpose of which is to convey a fundamental or a moral truth. Its content may or may not be based upon an historical event. Whether there was an event in time which might be called "the creation," or whether the physical components of the universe have always existed and time is infinite in extent, is not known. In any case there is an evolutionary process in which during the past several billion years simple components have been changing into more complex ones (for example the development of man from a single celled creature.) This means that the details of the Genesis creation myth must not be taken literally. Nor should they be forced into an artificial form, for example assuming that each day in the creation story stands for a million years. The details of the myth probably were never intended to be taken literally even by their author. They do reflect the belief that the Hebrews in the 9th century B. C. had about the structure of the universe. This idea is called a world-view, and the world-view of these early Hebrews was that the earth was a flat disc over which was fixed a bubble of air. The disc and the bubble were surrounded by water which extended for the greatest imaginable distance in all directions. The disc was called the earth, the bubble was called the firmament, and the water was called the Great Deep. Following is a sketch of this scheme:

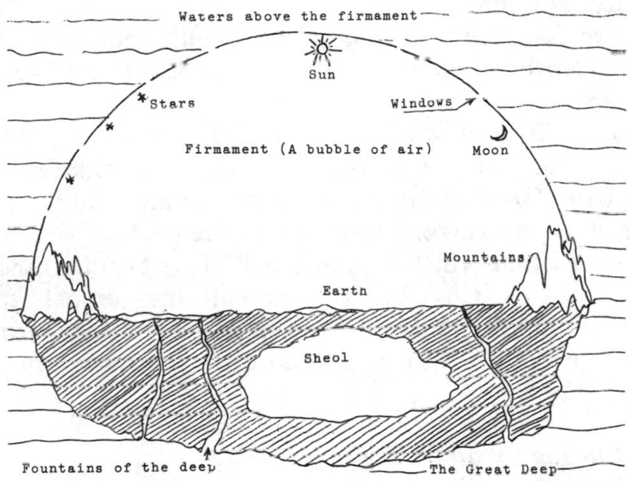

The Great Deep was thought to be connected in some physical way with the sea.[1] The Hebrews were never a sea-faring race and had a fear of or aversion to this terrifying unknown. They assumed that it was inhabited by an incarnation of evil. This creature was a sea-serpent and it had several names, viz., Rahab, Leviathan, and "the serpent."[2]

This theme is universal and has been carried out in many cultures. For example the serpent in the Garden of Eden represented an incarnation of evil. In the Middle Ages sailors were afraid of sea monsters. The conquest of evil is expressed in the fable of St. George and the dragon. Even today there is a great amount of interest and controversy over the Loch Ness "monster."

So much for the literal and physical aspects of the creation myth. We have said that the essential meaning of the story lies in the realm of moral truth. The fundamental truth is that God is the cause of the existence of all things. There are several aspects of this truth which become apparent when one reads the first two chapters of Genesis. They are as follows:

1. Everything that God creates is good. Since God is good and all knowing, this is an inevitable consequence of his activity. Evil is an alien intruder whose origin is a perversion of God's initial good. The possibility of such perversion arises in man's freedom to act as a co-creator and co-custodian of the good universe into which God has brought him.
2. Man is so structured physiologically that he works most efficently when every seventh day is a day of rest and of worship.
3. God did not create the universe *ex-nihilo,* or out of nothing, but he used the only material available, the water of the Great Deep, the home of evil incarnate. Hence God is able to overcome evil and to create that which is good out of that which supports evil. This becomes the central theme of Christianity wherein the unjust trial and subsequent murder of the Son of God is, through the Resurrection, turned into an event by which all men can be saved.

B. P and J in the Creation Myth

The creation myth cannot be entirely separated from the myth of Adam and Eve. In general, the creation theme is assumed to lie between Genesis 1:1 and 2:24. It is immediately apparent that this material consists of two accounts of the same event. The order of creation differs as well as the details of the orgin of man and woman. This is due to the fact that the section between 1:1 and 2:4 was written by the Priestly School, while 2:5 through 2:24 is attributable to J. This is a good point to become familiar with the idea that the material in the Bible is not arranged chronologically. P's account of the beginning of things was in part one of the last sections to be written.

[1] For the Hebrews this was the Mediterranean which they called the Great Sea.
[2] Cf. Psalm 89:10, Isaiah 27:1, Amos 9:3.

Chapter IV

ADAM AND EVE

"Adam" and "Eve" are approximate transliterations of the Hebrew words for "a man" and "a woman." Alexander Pope (1688-1744) wrote:

> "Know then thyself, presume not God to scan,
> The proper study of mankind is man."

The J source in Genesis (who wrote the story of Adam and Eve) had already gone beyond Pope with the conviction that neither God nor man could be understood at all unless something was known about the relationship between them.

The myth of Adam and Eve is not a story about a man named Adam and a woman named Eve who lived in a garden called Eden. It is a myth – a story the main purpose of which is to convey a moral truth. It is about every man and every woman who lives upon the earth, that is to say within the home that God has prepared for them. This home is the earth, and in the Gensis story it is represented as a garden or a park. It is a story about you.

The story is primitive. The naive, anthropomorphic style of J can be clearly seen. The principal subject of the story is profound, just as the questions of small children are sometimes profound. In a way, it tries to explain too many things, and so the main theme can be easily lost. For example, this myth attempts to account for the pain of childbirth, the source of the four best known rivers in the ancient Middle East, the reason why snakes are detested, and why farmers have to cope with the perversity of weeds.

The essential point of the story is to attempt an account for the existence of evil in the world. If God is all-good and everything that he made is good; and if God is all powerful, so that he created and sustains all things (as the creation myth has stated), why then do things exist that are evil and that are opposed to God?

J is suggesting the outlines of an answer. He postulates that God created man in his own image, presumably because companionship and communication is an essential component for higher forms of life. Man is given the godlike faculties of reason, creativity, and moral awareness. Furthermore he is given authority over those forms of life less complex than he. This is the significance of God's asking man to name the various animals. The Hebrew felt that to know the name of a person or an object gave the knower power over that whose name he knows.[1] Man is commanded to be fruitful and multiply. He, like God, is a creator and a responsible custodian of the world in which he lives.

The trouble begins when man is tempted to act as though he were equal to God. To eat of the fruit of the tree of the knowledge of good and evil means essentially to become the possessor of all knowledge – not the knowledge of right and wrong (for the myth implies that man already had that, as he was made in the image of God). The forbidden knowledge was technical knowledge. Knowledge that would enable him to design and calculate, to devise and formulate, to experiment and perfect any device that his mind could conceive. Some of these objects would be instruments of good and others instruments of evil.

The author of the Adam and Eve myth had one other essential factor in mind, and that is pride. Man was not satisfied with his dominion "over the fish of the sea, and over the birds of the air, and over the cattle, and over all the earth. . . . " He had also to "become like one of us" – godlike. He had to impose his own plans rather than to govern in trust that which was given to him under God's law. He went on to impose himself upon other men. He finally made God in his own image. And so man built a hothouse in which he planted seeds of military aggression, claims of theological infallibility, atheistic philosophies, and political corruption. Then he went on to use the forbidden knowledge to advance his own plans. It ought also to be noticed that the use of this previously forbidden knowledge introduced feelings of guilt.

And so, God, faced with this perversion of his original plan, denied man the right to perpetuate himself. He denied forever the ability of man to impose his plans upon God's plans. Man is denied access to the tree of eternal life. This gift of life is still obtainable, but not by pride and man's own efforts. The solution to the problem is offered in the New Testament.[2] It is offered in terms of a new agreement between God and man. It is not for the proud, but for the humble, the poor in spirit, the merciful, the pure in heart, the peacemakers. It is offered to those who accept Jesus as Lord.

[1] Cf. The story of Rumplestiltskin.
[2] The Hebrews never developed a doctrine of eternal life.

Chapter V

THE RESULTS OF DISOBEDIENCE

A. Cain and Abel

A part of the moral truth of the Adam and Eve myth is that disobedience to the law of God leads to unpleasant consequences. The last three myths in Genesis develop this idea. Let us consider first the story of Cain and Abel. Its author is J, but it is probably based on an ancient oral tradition which he received. Parts of the myth are obscure and difficult to interpret. As always, it is important to be aware of the dangers of literalism. In fact we find within this myth certain elements of an allegory.

Cain is a farmer and represents the elements of some ancient agricultural community. Abel is a shepherd and stands for the nomadic way of life. There has always been contention between shepherds and farmers over the use of land.[1] There was strife between Cain and Abel.

The author favors Abel. In the story God has regard for him and his offering. Since J is a Hebrew from the south of Palestine, the story may well reflect the ancient contention between the nomadic Hebrews as they moved into land occupied and farmed by the Canaanites. It is likely that the words Cain and Canaan have a common origin. However, the first contact between the nomadic, Semitic tribes which migrated from Mesopotamia was possibly as early as 2000 B. C. These nomads were not able to dislodge the Canaanites. This was 1150 years before J wrote the story of Cain and Abel. By the time J wrote, the Hebrews were long established in Palestine. Hence our supposition that the origin of the story was an oral source which reflected conditions long before 850 B. C.

At the close of the myth J writes "To Seth (Adam's son) also a son was born, and he called his name Enosh. At that time men began to call upon the name of Yahweh." We shall see later that it is probable that the Hebrews began to worship their God as Yahweh during the time of Moses (c. 1250 B. C.). This means that J (who uses the name Yahweh in referring to God) is reading the introduction of Yahweh's name back to the beginning of Hebrew history, some 750 years before the time of Moses.

The reference to the blood of Abel crying to Yahweh out of the ground stems from the Hebrew belief that blood was the carrier of life. It and life were sacred to them. Hence the prohibitions against eating meat with blood in it. This belief also led to the act of sprinkling blood on the altar during sacrifice as a symbolic act of the offering of a life to God.

There are two basic moral truths which this myth conveys. One is in the implied answer to Cain's question, "Am I my brother's keeper?" Yahweh's wish is that every man act out of the conviction that he has a responsibility towards everyone that his life touches. The second and more obvious truth is that jealousy and anger may lead to murder.

B. Noah and the Ark

The narrative structure of the myth of Noah is a mixture of the J source and the Priestly Source. Since we have found that J has presented a consistent theological outlook concerning the relationship between God and man, it is helpful if the J source alone be considered in reading the Noah story. It is found as follows: Gen. 5:29; 6:1-8; 7:1-5, 7, 10, 12, 16b, 22, 23, 8:2b, 3a, 6-12, 13b, 20-22. If the style and content of J alone is compared with the remainder of the narrative in which it is embedded, the marked differences which were pointed out on page 9 can be clearly seen.

Our original definition of myth said that its content might or might not be based on historical events as well as upon moral precepts. The Noah myth has some historical basis. Archaeological evidence shows that several cities in the Tigris-Euphrates valley have been inundated by severe floods at various times. A bed of clay 8 feet thick has been discovered at the site of the Babylonian city of Ur. Implements dug from the strata above and below the clay show it to be a deposit laid down by a tremendous flood probably in the third millenium B. C. Furthermore Babylonian records, as well as a remarkable piece of Babylonian folklore, all dating somewhere near 2000 B. C. make mention of a vast flood. The folklore, called the Gilgamesh Epic, recounts the story of its hero's search for eternal life. The details of the story are identical in many major points with the Noah myth. The most likely explanation is that J's account of the flood was a refinement of an oral tradition which came to the Hebrews either through the Amorites, who were Semitic nomads living on the borders of Mesopotamia and in Palestine, or as a result of the early Semitic tribes (the ancestors of Abraham) living in Babylonia.

Some of the features of the Noah myth that deserve special mention are as follows:

Chap. 6:1-2,4 This is a universal and ancient component of all mythology, viz. that there are special, semidivine creatures (kings, high-priests, messiah-figures) whose origin comes from the union of a god and a mortal.

Chap. 6:3 "120 years." Numerology had great significance for many ancient peoples (and for superstitious modern ones). "40" meant many, cf. Gen. 7:4,12. "Three" was a complete or perfect number for many cultures. It suggests completeness in such combinations as "morning, noon, night," "beginning, middle, end," "sun, moon, stars," and "earth, sea, sky." The combination of "completeness" and "many" (3 x 40=120) may have meant to the author that a life of 120 years was one complete and "full of days."

Chap. 6:5-7 The idea that such universal destruction, such as a large flood would bring, was God's punishment for man's evil was apparently new with the Hebrews. Other early flood-accounts did not give a moral reason for the devastation.

Chap. 7:2-4 The number "seven" was significant in ancient

cultures. It had a religious significance and also carried the connotation of completeness [cf. seven days in the week, and 3 + 4 (also a number with many sacred connotations) = 7].

The Noah myth was also written principally to bear witness to moral truths. It continues the idea introduced in the story of Adam and Eve that disobedience leads to unpleasant consequences. It is saying that God cares about right conduct. But as God made garments of skins to clothe Adam and Eve in their nakedness, and as he put a mark on Cain lest any who came upon him should kill him, so he promised Noah, "While the earth remains, seedtime and harvest, cold and heat, summer and winter, day and night, shall not cease." J is saying that God's mercy is greater than his desire for justice.

C. The Tower of Babel

The last of J's five myths has an affinity with the Noah story. It also is based in part on historical fact. There was a constant migration from the steppes around the Fertile Crescent into the Tigris-Euphrates valley, and then eastward across the Crescent to Palestine. Some of these tribes were nomandic Semites who were the earliest precursors of what was to become the Hebrew Commonwealth. Furthermore, the Sumerians, Akkadians, and Babylonians – early inhabitants of the plain between the two rivers – built towers of brick as places of worship. They were called ziggurats, and offered the worshipper an altar nearer to heaven than any built upon the plain.

By the time that J wrote, the Hebrews were involved in a long-continuing struggle against the worship of foreign gods. Since some foreign gods were worshipped on ziggurats, this practice became a natural focus against which J was writing. (Note that Babel and Babylon have the same root). However, he was able to do more than merely condemn the worship of gods other than Yahweh upon man-made hills. He also wrote against men presumptuously taking action together without reference to God's plan. This leads to their downfall and their further separation (sin) from other men. J states parenthetically that God's action in scattering the men who were trying to become as gods was the cause of the origin of various languages.

And so in the last of the five myths J throws light on the same theological theme – the separation of man and God – but from a different direction and hence producing different emphases.

[1]Cf. The difficulty caused by the Enclosure Movement in England in the 16th century.

Chapter VI

LEGEND IN GENESIS

A. Introduction

A legend is a story, the main purpose of which is to discuss the origins of a tribe or race. A legend always has some basis in history, but the story is not therefore to be taken categorically as literally true. Generally speaking only parts of it are factual in a literal sense. The rest is a mixture of symbolism, folklore, allegory, and myth.[1] There are four legends in Genesis, viz. those of Abraham, Isaac, Jacob, and Joseph. The authors are J, E, and P whose accounts have been interwoven by an editor a short time after 450 B. C.

B. Abraham

There was a constant flow of nomadic people into the Fertile Crescent from the ring of mountains to the north and the grassy steppes to the south. For the most part those migrating from the south were Semites. This means that they were tribes who spoke various Semitic dialects,[2] they were not a race. Those migrants from the Zagros Mountains in the north (Kassites, Hurrians, Mittani, Elamites) spoke either Indo-European dialects or languages peculiar to themselves. This migration into the Fertile

Crescent began in the fourth Millennium B. C. It continued into the first millennium and was accompanied by increasing pressures and warfare within the Crescent itself.

Around 2000 B. C. the powerful Amorite Kingdom of Amurra, with its capital at Mari, pushed east and captured the last Sumerian Kingdom, the 3rd dynasty of Ur. The Amorites merged with the Sumerians and Akkadians. At the same time another migration of nomadic Amorite tribes was in progress westward, across and out of the Fertile Crescent into Palestine, where the Canaanites already had existed as an established culture since 2500 B. C.

The legend of Abraham concerns events which occurred c. 2000 B. C. This means that even though Abraham was an historical person, the events behind the story also apply to pre-Israelite tribes. Some scholars regard Abraham as a legendary figure who stands for a typical (or the first) early Semitic, nomadic, Amorite tribe which migrated from the region around Haran in Mesopotamia to Canaan between 2000 and 1700 B. C.[3] It is extremely important to keep the fact in mind that the Hebrews did not worship one God whom they knew as Yahweh until the time of Moses, c. 1250 B. C. From 2000-1700 B. C., i. e. the Patriarchal Age, the Hebrew Commonwealth did not exist. There were only what might be called pre-Isaelite, Semitic, Amorite tribes which migrated from Mesopotamia into Canaan and Egypt. The legends concerning these tribes are the stories of Abraham, Isaac, Jacob and Joseph. Whom then did these tribes worship, what god called Abraham[4] from Haran to Canaan, and with whom did he make the covenant? The fact that the Lord is described in Genesis 18 as appearing to Abraham in the form of three men, the fact that Rachel stole her father's household gods before she fled with Joseph (cf. Gen. 31:19b), and the fact that many names in the patristic legends are combinations of El, the basic Semitic word for God,[5] all indicate that these tribes worshipped local or tribal Semitic gods.

Although the specific call of Abraham and the establishment of the convenant is ascribed by J, E. and P to Yahweh, this is clearly a reading-back into the story of a later concept. There is no essential theological difficulty here, however, for both Christian and Jew who now worship the same monotheistic God can say that this God influenced Abraham in some way, under some name, and so began the migrating coalescence of tribes which eventually would form the Hebrew nation.

There are several important stories within the Abraham legend that require special comment. They are as follows:

1. The fact that *Abraham* may well have represented the name of a tribe, or a region settled by a tribe can be seen from the fact that the names of the members of his geneology are in some cases also the names of regions or cities.

The geneology is as follows:

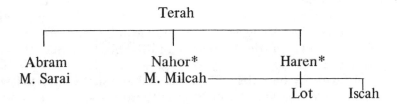

Terah

Abram
M. Sarai

Nahor*
M. Milcah

Haren*

Lot — Iscah

*Also place names

2. Compare Gen. 12:10-20, 20:1-18, and Gen. 26:1-11. This is essentially the same story told once about Abraham and Sarai and once about Isaac and Rebekah. Such a pair is called a doublet. This event may have happened to either Abraham or Isaac, but in retelling, the characters became the source of confusion and only the plot remained.
3. Gen. 19:30-38. The Hebrews hated the Moabites and the Ammonites. Hence J defames their origin. Note once again that Moab and Ammon are used interchangeably for people and nations.
4. Gen. 22, The Testing of Abraham. This story is from the E source. It was written to show that even though the nations surrounding Israel practiced human sacrifice (often killing children), Yahweh does not require this kind of worship.

C. Isaac

The legend of Isaac reflects that period when Amorite tribes which were eventually to form the Hebrew nation were beginning to settle in Canaan and became exclusivistic with regard to Canaanites. Hence the importance of Isaac taking his wife

Rebekah from the midst of his native people near Nahor in Mesopotamia.

The story of Jacob and Esau is legendary in the true sense of the word in that it attempts to explain the conditions under which the Edomites and the Israelites[6] originated. The elements of an allegory are also present.

In the story Esau is the archetypal ancestor of the Edomites. This follows from the fact that the Hebrew word for *red* is *Edom.* Esau was red when he was born, and he traded his birthright for red pottage. Jacob is the archetypal ancestor of the Hebrew tribes in Palestine. The fact that Esau was born first reflects the Hebrews acknowledgment that the Edomites were an older nation than the Hebrews. The struggle within the womb stands for the ancient struggle between the Edomites and the nomadic Semitic ancestors of the Hebrews.

However, the older of two nations is usually invested with the honor due to longevity, just as the firstborn son is accorded special privileges. The author of the legend (J and E) felt the need to deny the Edomites claim to such honor, and to assert the superiority of the Hebrews. Jacob won the birthright by being more clever than Esau and so established his superiority. We might think that this was a dishonorable kind of trickery, but to the Semite this was more on the order of a shrewd bargain. The same theme is repeated, only this time with the blessing of Isaac as the prize, in Gen. 27.

D. Jacob

The legend of the third patriarch shows the continued importance of exclusivism among certain Semitic tribes living in Palestine. The purity of ancestry is kept uncontaminated as Jacob returns to Mesopotamia for his wives Rachel and Leah. The portrayal of Jacob as a shrewd man is continued. As a result of his diligence he becomes more wealthy and so more despised by his father-in-law Laban. Laban was an Aramean. Perhaps the story meant to show that the Hebrews were superior in bargaining to the Arameans. In the time of the authorship of J and E the Arameans were establishing their power in Damascus and increasingly were enemies of the Hebrews.

Jacob, on the other hand, is not portrayed as a totally good man. The account of his wrestling with God (his conscience) in Chapter 32, and the subsequent change in his character, shows J's realization for the constant need of moral reform of the nation.

Chapter 34 is important for our later understanding of the steps which took place in the formation of the Hebrew Commonwealth. Shechem is the name of an ancient Canaanite city, and in the story Shechem is the archetype of a Canaanitic tribe. The story indicates that the pre-Israelite tribes were unwilling to intermarry with other Semitic tribes, but that there existed a moral awareness among some of them which caused them to condemn the tribes of Simeon and Levi for their treacherous act. As a result of this feeling Simeon and Levi were probably driven out of the area of Shechem south to the Sinai peninsula.

Genesis 35:23-26 lists the names of the twelve sons of Jacob, which in turn are the names of the twelve tribes of Israel. However, there is disagreement in various parts of the Old Testament over the names of the tribes. There is only agreement over the number twelve. In all probability there were many tribes, most of whose names have been lost to us. The fact that the number twelve became important appears to be an artificial stricture introduced for the sake of the special importance that the number had for Hebrews. This symbolism has been carried over into the New Testament where the twelve apostles of the New Israel replace the twelve tribes of the Old Israel.

E. Joseph

In the legend of Joseph it is virtually impossible to separate tribal history from biographical material. In any event it is a good story, which may account for its preservation in such detail. It has the overtones of a myth in that it conveys a moral which is found in Gen. 50:19,20 – "But Joseph said to them (his brothers), "Fear not, for am I in the place of God? As for you, you meant evil against me; but God meant it for good, to bring it about that many people should be kept alive, as they are today."

Many scholars feel that not all the Semitic tribes which would eventually form the Hebrew nation were in Egypt, but that only two were there, viz. Ephraim and Manasseh.[7] The details of the Exodus suggest the involvement of a small number of people. When we consider the Kenite Hypothesis we shall see that two is the right number of tribes to have been in Egypt.

[1] In some cases the author draws a moral from the content of the legend. . . . These parts therefore are semi-mythical in character. An example is the Joseph legend which is strongly moralistic in tone.

[2] Some examples of Semitic languages are Akkadian, Babylonian, Assyrian, Amoritic, Canaanitic, Armaen, Arabic and Phoenician.

[3] Cf. Ezekiel 16:3 "Thus says the Lord God to Jerusalem: Your origin and your birth are of the land of the Canaanites; your father was an Amorite, and your mother a Hittite."

[4] Abram and Abraham are two linguistic variations of the same name, meaning *exalted father*. Abraham is probably the Aramaic form of the Amoritic *Abram*. The reason given in the narrative for the change of the name is probably P's attempt to explain its existence in two forms (cf. Gen. 17:5).

[5] Cf. Kemuel, Bethuel, Ishmael, Adbeal, Bethel, Ruel, etc.

[6] The term Israelite refers to a member of the Hebrew nation sometime after its formation c. 1250 B. C.

[7] Joseph's sons

Chapter VII

MOSES, THE EXODUS, AND THE FORMATION OF THE HEBREW COMMONWEALTH

A. The Hebrews in Egypt

From the time that "There arose a new king over Egypt, who did not know Joseph" [Exodus 1:8], until the Exodus under Moses, the Hebrews in Egypt did not prosper. The dates between these events are not easy to determine. More is known about events in Egypt as described in the account of the Exodus than is known from the situation as it is described in the Joseph legend. For example, Pharaoh Merneptah erected a stele c. 1220 B.C. describing a victory over the "people of Israel" in Palestine. Therefore, the Exodus must have occurred a sufficient time before that to allow for the Exodus and the beginning of the conquest of Canaan.

In addition it is known that the building of the store cities of Pithom and Raamses (and the transfer of the capital from Thebes to Raamses) were part of the plan of the Nineteenth Dynasty (c. 1310-1200) to conquer and control Palestine. A consideration of all the archaeological and Biblical evidence postulates the date of the Exodus in the reign of Ramses II c. 1250 B. C. Taking this as a base and going back to Joseph in accordance with Exodus

12:40 [the time that the people of Israel dwelt in Egypt was four hundred thirty years], one arrives at a date for Joseph's influence in Egypt of c. 1680 B. C. This places Joseph's administration well into the period of Hyksos domination [c. 1720-1570 B. C.]. This in effect is the only time that Joseph could have found favor in the court of Pharaoh since he would have been a Semite in a Semitic regime. Furthermore, the capital of Egypt in Joseph's day was Avaris (Tanis), near Goshen.[1]

Little is known of this interim period of Hyksos domination. It interrupted a long unbroken line of indigenous Egyptian rule. The Hyksos were Semitic invaders from Palestine as shown by the documents of this period, which list Semitic names. They were able to conquer Egypt because of their introduction of the horse and war chariot, the compound bow, and a new style of ramp fortification. The Egyptians adopted these innovations.

After the expulsion of the Hyksos by Ahmose (c. 1570-1545 B.C.), the Hebrews must have fallen into disfavor. Their plight worsened until their deliverance by Moses began a chain of events which not only brought them out of Egypt but introduced them to their ultimate and final God, Yahweh.

B. Moses

The details of Moses' birth are found in Exodus 1:1-10. However, the same story was told about Sargon I, king of Akkad, in the late twenty-fourth century B.C., some 1400 years before the birth of Moses. The Mesopotamian cunieform inscription reads as follows:

> "My vestal mother conceived me, in secret she brought me forth,
> She set me in a basket of rushes, with bitumen she closed my door,
> She cast me into the river, which rose not over me.
> The river bore me up, unto Akki the irrigator it carried me.
> Akki the irrigator lifted me out.
> Akki the irrigator as his own son reared me.
> Akki the irrigator as his gardener appointed me."

The reason for the similarities in the two stories is simply that by the time Moses had become a great man the details of his ordinary birth and childhood were forgotten. By Moses' time the Sargon story may have become a hero-epic which was thought to be suitable for attribution to Moses because the roots of what was to become the Hebrew nation went back to Abraham in Mesopotamia. In fact, so great had become Moses' stature that the total contents of the first five Books of the Old Testament [The Pentateuch], because of their legal content were ascribed to his authorship. It is obvious, however, that his involvement was limited to the earliest Hebrew encounter with Yahweh, and probably no more of the law codes than that part which is contained in the Ten Commandments.

C. The Kenite Hypothesis

The authors E and P refrain from referring to God as *Yahweh* until after describing Moses' encounter with God at the burning of the bush in Sinai. This may reflect an old tradition that after this time the Hebrews worshipped God under this new name. The Kenite hypothesis is one attempt to explain how the worship of Yahweh by the Hebrews originates. This theory assumes that the Semitic, nomadic, pre-Israelitic tribes which emigrated westward across the Fertile Crescent in the Patriarchal Age, worshipped household gods, as well as the chief gods of Mesopotamia or of whatever country they resided in.[2]

When Moses fled from Egypt to escape the wrath of Pharaoh, he went to the Sinai peninsula where he lived with a tribe of coppersmiths known as Kenites.[3] He married the daughter of the high-priest of this tribe and hence became closely involved in the worship of the God of the Kenites. This god was a storm god of the mountains[4] whose name was Yahweh. [cf. also Exodus 18:1-10-12].

D. YHWH

Hebrew is a Semitic language. It is written from right to left because the early inscriptions were engraved in stone with a hammer and chisel. Such a process is carried out more easily by a right-handed man from right to left. Originally, there were no vowels and the language was based on tri-literal consonantal roots. The name Yahweh appears in Hebrew as HWHY[5] יהוה[6] The root is HWH. This is a very basic and fundamental form which appears in many words, in several Near Eastern languages, with many connotations. Each one alludes to one of the Hebrew concepts of the nature of God.

One of the meanings of the root is "to be" or "to happen" or "to cause to be." He who always is is eternal. He who causes to be is a creator. Other connotations of the root are "he who causes to fall" or "he who causes to blow." These carry allusions to a storm god who causes lightning to fall and the wind to blow, or perhaps to a fertility god who causes rain to fall. There is also a connection between wind and spirit [ruach], breath, and life. Which of these many ideas the Hebrews associated with the word Yahweh can never be known.

E. Sinai and Beyond

The Kenite hypothesis proposes that only the Joseph tribes [Ephraim and Manasseh] were involved in the Exodus. Their number must have been relatively small, perhaps around 2,000. The evidence for this is indirect, but it involves the following: (1) the Hebrews were ministered to in Egypt by only two midwives in Exodus 1:15, (2) the escape from Egypt was so well coordinated, (3) Aaron was able to speak to all the refugees as they stood together in Exodus 16:10, and (4) the fact that a desert such as Sinai could not support a large number of people living together.[6]

The Kenite hypothesis further supposes that at the time the Joseph tribes were escaping from Egypt, there were both Israelite and concubine[7] tribes living in central Palestine, and that the Semitic tribes of Simeon and Levi and Judah were living near the Kenites in Sinai. Simeon and Levi had been driven out of the region of Shechem southward as described by the tribal legend of Dinah in Genesis 34. After the Joseph tribes, the Kenites, Simeon, Levi, and Judah had been amalgamated under the leadership of Moses, they formed a federation which was held together both by the new law received and transmitted by Moses (the Ten Commandments), and by the worship of the god Yahweh. This amalgamation took a generation (forty years) to complete during nomadic migrations in the region of Sinai. Finally these tribes moved northward, and under the military leadership of Joshua entered central Palestine where the amalgamation was eventually completed by the addition of Israelite and concubine tribes to the confederation. The conquest of Canaan was a long, slow process that took two hundred years to complete. It was not always a concerted effort, but was often the affair of an individual tribe (cf. Judges 1). Its climax is described in Joshua 24. Joshua's appeal for a unified worship of Yahweh shows that even as late as the period of the conquest of Canaan under the Judges (c. 1150 B. C.) the various Semitic tribes were still worshipping the collection of gods which had been accumulated during the long migratory history between 2000 B. C. and 1150 B. C. This pantheon included the gods of Mesopotamia, Canaan, Egypt, and Sinai.

[1]Cf. Gen. 46:28: "He sent Judah before him to Joseph, to appear before him in Goshen; and they came into the land of Goshen."

[2]Cf. Joshua 24:2. And Joshua said to all the people, "Thus says the Lord, the God of Israel, 'Your fathers lived of old beyond the Euphrates, Terah, the father of Abraham and of Nahor; and they served other gods.' "

[3]It is assumed that the Kenites were living among the Midianites at this time because:

1. The Kenites are descendents of Moses' father-in-law. Cf. Judges 4:11.
2. The Kenites helped the Joseph tribe escape from Egypt and entered Palestine with the tribe of Judah. Cf. 1 Sam. 15:6.

[4]Cf. Judges 5.

[5]Called the tetragrammaton.

[6]Numbers 1:46 gives the number of the refugees in Sinai as 603,550. This may be because the numerical equivalent of all the Hebrew letters in the phrase "Sum all people Israel" is 603,550.

[7]Half Semitic, half Canaanitic.

CHAPTER VIII

Judges[1]

I. The Literary Sources of Judges.

The Book of Judges describes the conquest of Canaan. This conquest took place roughly between the time of the emergence of the Hebrew tribes from Sinai under the leadership of Joshua (c. 1200 B. C.) until the establishment of a pre-monarchy under Saul (c. 1050 B. C.). The subjugation of the Canaanites was not a concerted and completely successful campaign conducted under the leadership of one man (viz. Joshua). The conquest was largely an effort of individual tribes (or of coalitions of a few tribes) in isolated and widely separated areas. The Hebrews incurred defeats as well as victory. Some areas of Canaan were never subdued. The most notable example is the Philistine plain.[2]

The account of Hebrew history as it appears in Judges represents a collation of several authors, as was true of previous Biblical material. There are five major literary sources discernable in Judges. They are as follows:

> J. These are local hero tales and stories of conquests by individual tribes in isolated areas. The author is called J. He may or may not be the J who contributed to the Pentateuch. His date is c. 850 B. C.

E. An author analogous to the E of the Pentateuch. His style is scarcely distinguishable from J. He wrote about local heroes. His date is c. 750 B. C.

RJE. "R" stands for redactor. He took the J and E accounts of local hero tales and isolated conquests and rewrote them as an idealized account of national history. His stories are difficult to distinguish from E's writing. For example, the stories of Gideon and Samson were independent local hero tales. They were combined with E material to form a connected history of Israel. For example, in the story of Gideon, the destruction of the Midianites is a national epic. However, Zebah and Zalmunna[3] were characters in a local story. RJE was a national historian who wrote c. 650 B. C.

RD. These initials stand for Deuteronomic redactor. This material is the work either of a school of writers or of an individual whose interest is religion. The author is a preacher-moralist. The Deuteronomic theme is developed that disobedience to Yahweh leads to destruction. Typical examples of this writing are Judges 8:33-35 and Judges 13:1. The date of RD is c. 550 B. C.

P. This author (or school) had the same interest as the Priestly School in the Pentateuch. He added a ritualistic emphasis c. 400 B. C. There is comparatively little of this content in Judges. One example is Judges 2:1-5.

II. The Song of Deborah (Judges 5)

A. The Song of Deborah is the oldest writing in the Bible. Its most probable date is c. 1100 B. C. It is a story of the united effort of several Hebrew tribes to win a military victory over the Canaanites. The notable aspects of the story are that some of the tribes did not join the coalition and that it gives support to the Kenite hypothesis.

B. The following facts should be noted about the story:

1. The following tribes were faithful to this pre-Israelite confederation against the Canaanites:

Naphtali
Issachar
Zebulun
Benjamin
Ephraim
Machir.

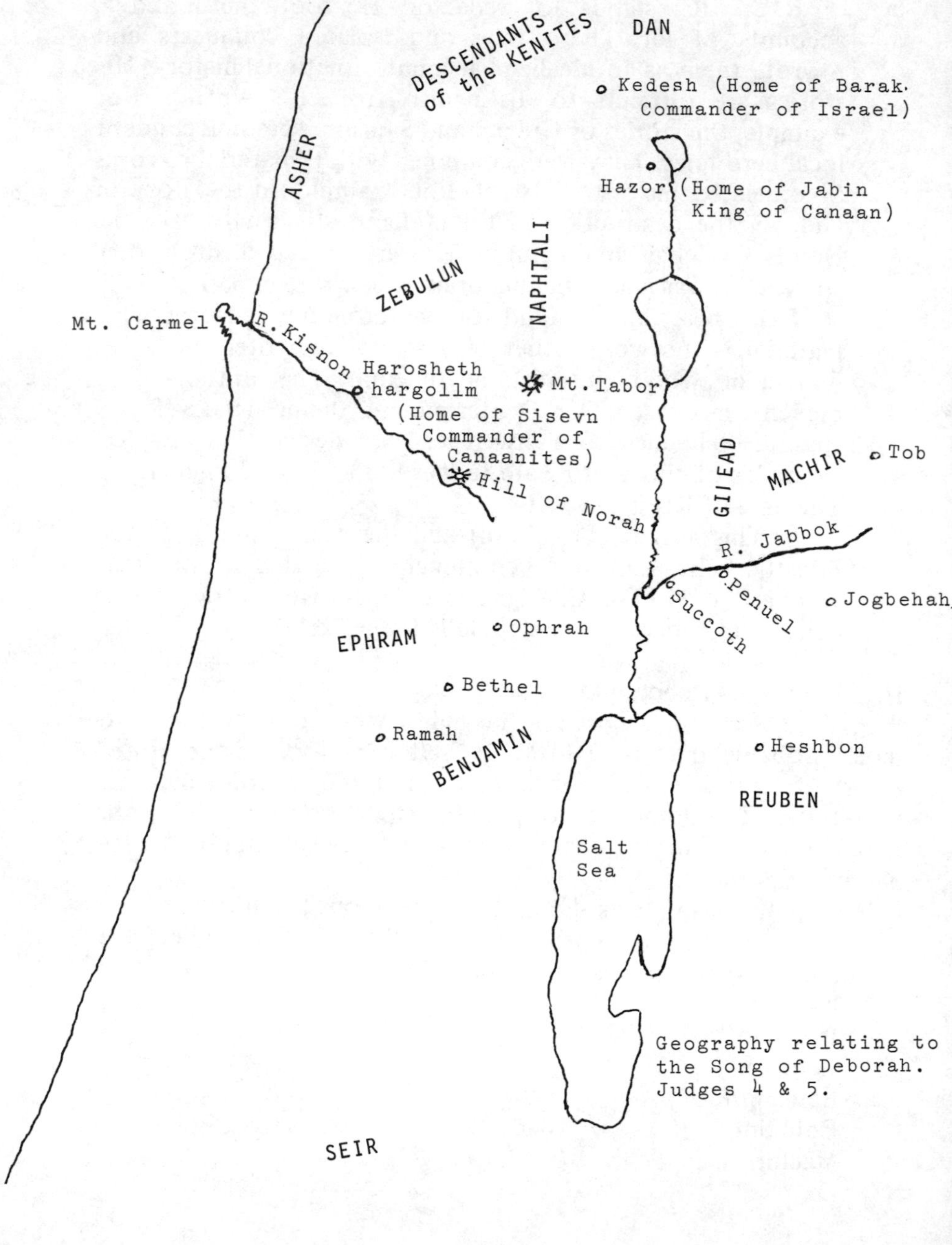

Geography relating to the Song of Deborah. Judges 4 & 5.

Naphtali, Issachar, and Zebulun were influenced to answer Deborah's call for help because of their geographical proximity (see map, page 42). The call to assembly was at Mount Tabor, the traditional gathering place for these three tribes. Ephraim and Benjamin answered the call because they were recent converts to the worship of Yahweh (Kenite hypothesis) and hence showed zeal for the coalition. These two tribes represent the core of the faithful tribes. Ephraim was in Egypt and Benjamin may have been. At least Benjamin's home was near Sinai and they met and helped the Joseph tribes when they left Egypt.

2. The following tribes were unfaithful:

Dan
Rueben
Asher
Gilead
Meroz

This is logical because these tribes were on the geographical fringe of the action. Dan and Asher were half Canaanitic (concubine tribes) and had little loyalty to Yahweh. Reuben in south trans-Jordania had little interest in the happenings in Samaria and Galilee.

3. Gilead and Meroz, which are mentioned as tribes in Judges 5, are not mentioned at all in J's tribal lists.

4. The following tribes are mentioned as Israelite tribes in J, but are not mentioned at all in Judges 5:

Gad
Simeon
Levi
Judah
Manasseh

This means that no accurate list of the names of the actual tribes has survived. Only the ritual number 12 is of importance and has come down to us.

5. Judah is not mentioned because it was formed later out of an amalgam of Simeon, Levi, and the Kenites. Simeon and Levi were weak because of their decimation at Shechem. Their lack of interest may have been due to their adulteration by the Kenites. Even though the Kenites did introduce Yahweh to the Israelites, they did not have the ancestral tie to Abraham and so lacked the commitment of the other Hebrew

tribes.

6. In the story Yahweh comes up from Kadesh[4], his mountain home in Sinai, to help the Israelites. He is a storm god and a war god, who floods the Kishon with a deluge of rain, causing it to overflow onto the Plain of Esdraelon, bogging the chariots of the Canaanites.

7. This poem makes the claim that is to become the theme of the Deuteronomist and of the prophets, namely that devotion to Yahweh will bring success (in this case military success) and life to the nation.

8. "From the heaven fought the stars, from their courses they fought against Sisera." 5:20. This is saying that not only Yahweh, but all the workings of the universe are on the side of the just.

Some questions for review:
1. How much can you see of the religious, national, and historical philosophy of the Hebrews in this poem?
2. What features make it likely that this was written by an eye witness to the event?
3. What does it say about the conquest of Canaan by the Hebrews?
4. What does it say about the Hebrews as a nation in 1100 B. C.?
5. If this is the earliest writing in the Bible, why isn't it Genesis 1:1?

[1] The judges mentioned in this Book are:

Othniel	Jair
Ehud*	Jephthah*
Shamgar	Ibzan
Deborah*	Elon
Gideon*	Abdon
Abimelech*	Samson*
Tola	

Those of importance are marked with an asterisk.

[2] For the true picture of the nature of the conquest read:

a. Judges I.

b. Joshua 15:13b-19, 63. (cf. esp. v. 63).

"But the Jebusites, the inhabitants of Jerusalem, the people of Judah could not drive out; so the Jebusites dwell with the people of Judah at Jerusalem to this day."

c. Joshua 17:11-18.

d. Joshua 19:47.

"When the territory of the Danites was lost to them, the Danites went up and fought against Leshem (a Canaanite city), and after capturing it and putting it to the sword they took possession of it and settled in it, calling Leshem, Dan, after the name of Dan their ancestor."

[3] Cf. Judges 8:4-21.

[4] Or Horeb, or Sinai, or Seir.

Chapter IX

SOCIAL AND POLITICAL ORGANIZATION IN ISRAEL DURING JOSHUA/JUDGES (c. 1200 – 1100 B. C.)

A. Tribal Organization

The social organization of the Middle East is and always has been vertical – that is to say – loyalties remain within a tribal or family structure. There is no possibility of effective international agreements such as those seen among the Communist nations (China being the present exception). Nor is there a chance for nationalism to emerge as a strong controlling force. Nasser is the best example of a nationalist leader in the Near East, and he is far from a deGaulle. The Arab League which consists of 70,000,000 members cannot organize effectively enough to crush 2,000,000 Jews in Palestine whom they hate and whose territory they believe belongs to the Arabs.

This tribal organization probably had its origin in the fact that existence in the Ancient Middle East tended to be nomadic. The number of people who can survive while using the resources of an inhospitable terrain are limited, and the members of a tribe must unite as a security against nature and other tribes who are involved in the same struggle for survival. This requirement of protectiveness found a special expression in the treatment of women, who were veiled and set apart to live in women's tents (or even a screened off part of the sheik's tent). Although the women were subservient to the men and not allowed to participate in community decisions, their social role at the nerve center of the existence of tribal life was neither neglected or unimportant. For example, the women named the children. A name was all-important to a Hebrew, and considered to be a source of power and to be influential upon character.

In conjunction with this concern for the importance of the role of women in society we find that it was required of Hebrew men to marry only Semitic women, and eventually only those Semitic women who were members of an "in-group" who were in some way related to Abraham, Isaac, Jacob, and Joseph. The all-importance of the family group to the Hebrews is seen further in the fact that they of all the foreign nations did not condone prostitution, even at a time when their surrounding neighbor nations were encouraging "cult prostitution" as a holy, desirable, and acceptable activity.

Within this social structure the individual was subordinate to the group. Judgment, and decisions were placed in the hands of a few men, the tribal leader, or judge, and to the "old men who sat in the gate." This meant in a sense that the individual was sacrificed to the common good. This way of thinking emerges in two ways in later Hebrew culture. The idea of the sacrifice of one for many is precursive to a doctrine of the vicarious suffering of the Suffering Servant,[1] whereby one man is described as dying so that all men may live. It also contains the seeds of the idea of corporate personality – a belief that the life of one man is representative of the life of the whole and the whole nation somehow reflects the life of any one of its members. One example of this diffusion of personality is found in the custom that vengeance for murder could be lawfully carried out on *any* member of the tribe of the murderer.

Within the clan the elders were on a par. One reason for Israel's split after Solomon's rule was the insistence of one man (Rehoboam) in laying down the law, in spite of the advice of the elders against this high-handed policy. It had always been the custom to consult the elders before moving the tents, declaring war, or making peace.

This way of life included the conviction that people are more important than things. Wealth was secondary to the quality of a person's life for the Hebrew, hence it was shared – spoils were either divided after a battle, or burned because they were thought to be contaminated by the spirit of the enemy's god,[2] or the spoils were offered to Yahweh. There arose within the tribal structure of Israel in the 12th century B. C. the beginnings of the concept of brotherly action: a realization that men are interdependant but that they also must respect each other's freedom.

Tribal society was and is essentially conservative. The Hebrew word for "custom" is *mishpat* – this is what has always been done. This is "right conduct," hence it becomes important that things be done as in the past. Religion was practiced in a traditional way which became a fixed ritual. There was very little (or perhaps) no written law, but there was an established practice in almost every area of life. The stability of the past was retained without a written history or code of laws. As yet there was no concept of actions guided by a right inner spirit, but at least there was recognition of the existence of something more important than a written rule.

This spirit of conservatism grew to its climax in the area of moral interpretation when it became the foundation of the teaching of the prophets in the 8th century B. C. However, after Israel had gone through the Babylonian captivity (597 – 536 B. C.) the increase of the influence of the Temple priesthood marked the beginning of a harmful introversion and a narrowing interpretation of the law. This development was partly unavoidable since the increase in complexity of life which resulted in the change from a nomadic to an agricultural to an urban society complicated the application of *mishpat* to the point where three interpretations became necessary: prophetic, priestly and rabbinic.

During the period of Joshua/Judges there existed continual fighting among the Hebrew tribes.[3] However, the animosity was somewhat restricted in that an Israelite could not plunder his fellow tribesman; anyone else was fair game. Although it seemed unimportant at first, these feelings of tribe loyalty led to a feeling of Israelite nationalism which was combined with a feeling of exclusiveness as the elect and chosen people of Yahweh. This period marked the beginning of teaching about hospitality. The weak, widowed, orphans, and strangers were cared for.

B. Warfare

In this pre-monarchial period of Joshua and Judges the successful conduct of war by the Hebrews against the inhabitants of the land was a necessary prerequisite to the formation of a nation. This success often depended upon the concerted action of several tribes. The ability to act concertedly depended in turn upon the existence of a feeling of fellowship between the tribes involved. This feeling was equated with a holy or psychic force which infused the whole nation. It was a kind of *esprit de corps.* Yahweh was believed to be the source of this strength, therefore preparations for war were made accordingly.

Since Yahweh was the source of this spiritual power, the Hebrews looked for a unity of soul among their people (especially among the warriors).[4] Previous to battle, all efforts were directed towards creating and maintaining a state of unified psychic strength. Such strength was promoted by the purity resulting from ceremonial washing and ritual cleanliness (Judges 7:1). It was increased in a practical way by pardoning the timid, fearful, and newly married (presumably the distracted), from battle. Hence the chance that fear or panic would spread throughout the army was diminished. The warriors abstained from food, supposedly to sharpen the senses and as a kind of training rule. The implements of war were anointed with holy oil so that the spirit of Yahweh would soak into them.[5] Sacred objects were brought into the camp, in the belief that the presence of Yahweh came with them. The chief would make a promise to Yahweh in return for a guarantee of victory. For example, Jephthah promised the life of the first person who came out to meet him upon his return from battle with the Ammonites if he were to be victorious. This impulsive promise cost him the life of his daughter. Also, the leader of the tribe would usually consult a priest concerning the expediency of any warlike venture. The priest in turn would consult his ark or oracle box, drawing lots to guide his answer. Sometimes a curse was called down upon the psychic force of the enemy.[6] It was also customary to dedicate a part of the spoils of war to Yahweh so that they would not, through greed, corrupt the soul of the victors.

To a large degree war was psychological in this era. Jericho was captured after several days of silent but threatening maneuvers. Gideon was motivated to act as a result of a dream that a cake of barley tumbled into a Midianite tent and caused it to collapse.

When the ark of Yahweh was brought into the Israelite camp, the great shout that went up brought terror to their enemies, the Philistines. But when the Philistines captured the same ark (which was the home of Yahweh), the Israelites in turn became panic stricken.

Perhaps times have not changed greatly. The threat of the terror of nuclear war, and the fear that accompanies it, is perhaps the most significant factor in the cold war between the East and West.

C. Chieftain

Local chiefs or judges, such as Ehud, Deborah, Gideon, Abimelech, Jephthah, and Samson, held their positions by virtue of their possession of the Spirit *(Ruach)* of Yahweh. They had absorbed the divine soul. It was appointed to each in a different way. Samson was set apart by means of announcement of an angel to his mother (cf. Judges 13:3 ff.). Gideon was spoken to directly by the Lord (cf. Judges 6:11 ff.). Jepthah was called by the elders of Gilead.

The relationship between the chief and the members of his tribe varied. Samson, for example, went his own way and did as he pleased. Jephtah's authority was essentially an interim arrangement. In these early pre-monarchical days there was a freedom in the role of the chieftain that was never recaptured.

D. Holy Places and Holy Things.

Just as there were special people (judges, chiefs, priests, and prophets) who were filled with the strength of holiness (which in itself was an extension of the soul, or spirit, or breath, or *ruach* of Yahweh), so there were places which were marked by a concentration of holy strength. Mount Sinai was one of the earliest of these sacred locations. Canaan was filled with sanctuaries which were sacred to Canaanitic gods. These were appropriated by the Israelites as they conquered the land and were converted to repositories of Yahweh's spirit. This holy energy was thought to be active in wells and trees (i. e. in living and moving sources of life). It was also present in tombs since the strength and blessing of ancestors were present there. Stones were thought to have the ability to absorb and contain psychic energy. Early stone altars were built from unhewn rock, since these special stones were in a sense alive – infused with the holy power of Yahweh. To cut them would injure the psychic aspect of their existence.

Holiness was considered by the Hebrews to be a force that lay at the root of all kinds of energy. Life itself depended on it. It was considered the tie that bound all men and other beings to Yahweh. Holiness was that which increased the strength of the soul. This concept eventually lead to the isolation of Israel from the surrounding nations to preserve holiness from contamination through contact with foreign gods and ideals.

[1] This poem occurs in II Isaiah and was written c. 400 B. C.

[2] This total destruction was called *herem.*

[3] Gideon vs. Ephraim. Judges 7:24

[4] Cf. The Song of Deborah, Judges 5.

[5] As native hunters in Africa dip their spears into the blood of a slain lion in order to absorb his strength and courage.

[6] Cf. The story of Balaam and Balak, Num. 22.

Chapter X.

THE PROBLEM OF SYNCRETISM IN THE PERIOD OF JUDGES

A. Micah and the Danites.

The story of Micah and the Danites in chapters 17 and 18 of Judges clearly and briefly describes the religious and political situation in Palestine in the time of Judges.[1] It was possible for the leader of a tribe to have anyone he chose for a priest. First Micah chose his own son, then he replaced him with a Levite, since members of this tribe were thought to be slightly more preferable than anyone else as priests.

The tribe of Dan originally settled in Southern Palestine near Judah. The hostile Philistines were between the Danites and the shore of the Mediterranean Sea. The Philistines expanded eastward and drove the Hebrews out. The city of Laish which the Danites conquered was far to the north, inland from the Phoenician cities of Tyre and Sidon. In stealing Micah's priest and taking him with them, the worship of Yahweh was established in extreme northern Palestine.

B. Baal Worship

The established gods of the Canaanite culture were

"baals". The word "baal" means "lord." Each baal was lord of his own territory, which was usually limited in size. Baals were nature gods whose particular concern was with fertility, especially as it was exemplified in crop yield. Each baal had a female partner known as a "baalath" (lady) or "ashtoreth." The belief was held that the fertility of the soil, abundant rain, and good weather were dependent upon and associated with the sexual relationship between baal and ashtoreth. It was further assumed that the worship of the baals should naturally be centered in rites of a sexual nature. These rites were conducted by cult prostitutes who lived in shrines or temples which were built on hilltops (and hence nearer the gods). The practice of prostitution was supposed to create a sympathetic magic[2] which enhanced the fertility between baal and ashtoreth and then was reflected in a good yield at harvest time.

C. Yahweh Worship

These rites were repulsive to the classical and more conservative members of Judaism since they had already begun to develop a sense of morality which was expressed in part by fidelity between man and wife. The custom (mishpat) of worshipping only Yahweh, and the centrality of the Covenant made baal worship unacceptable to Hebrews who remained faithful to Yahweh. Unlike the fertility gods of Canaan, Yahweh, as the god of the Hebrews, was unique. He was the only god whose special care involved this group of Semites. Furthermore, Yahweh was a god of war and history. He was no longer primarily a nature god, even though his origins with the Kenites depict him as a storm god. Yahweh was worshipped in rites involving the sacrifice of animals and, within the context of the Covenant; by adopting its sign (circumcision) and by living in accordance with its terms (obedience to the law).

The sacrificial aspect of the worship of Yahweh was based upon the desire for atonement – the wish to have one's sins forgiven and to be reinstated with God, i. e. to be at one with him (at-one-ment). The Hebrews did not believe that sins could be erased – what is done is indelibly done. At most, these transgressions of the law could only be covered up. The Hebrew word *kaphar* means "to cover." Hence *Yom Kaphar* (Yom Kippur) is "the day to cover" sins. It is the day of atonement.

A ritual existed in earliest times which could be performed by anyone desiring to express symbolically this act of atonement. As time went on, it came to be reserved for the chief of a tribe, or head of a family, and was finally performed exclusively by priests. In its earlier form the ritual consisted of building an altar of earth or stone where the Spirit (Ruach) of Yahweh was believed to be localized. Then the sacrificer chose an animal (usually a lamb) without blemish. This symbolized a life of perfect innocence: perfect because the animal had no physical defects; innocence because animals do not know the difference between right and wrong and cannot sin. Let us call the man who is making the sacrifice offering "the sinner." The sinner leads the lamb to the altar – that is, they draw near to Yahweh. Then the sinner places his hands on the head of the animal. This act says in effect, "I identify myself with this beast. What happens to it physically stands for that which happens to me spiritually. It happens to my intangible being – my will, my thoughts, my hopes, my desires, my innermost self." Next he cuts the lamb's throat and sprinkles blood on the altar. Hebrews believed that the life was in the blood, just as the Greeks believed that it was in the breath. Hence man is offering his life to God.

A fire is lit on the altar symbolizing the presence of Yahweh.[3] The lamb, representing the sinner, is placed over the flames. Two things happen – he is changed, transformed by the power of Yahweh into a better state of being. At the same time, just as the smoke rises to heaven – "a pleasing odor, an offering by fire to the Lord" – so the transformed sinner raises himself to God and pleases God by his act of atonement. Finally, all who are present at the ceremony partake of the offering in a communal meal. Just as all are strengthened by the food, so are the lives of all men enriched who are touched by the life of him who was once a sinner but is now atoned.[4]

D. The Need for Syncretism

As the Hebrews infiltrated Canaan in the 12th century B. C., their nomadic existence gave way to a relatively settled agricultural economy. Hence the concept of Yahweh changed from a god of warfare and history to include that of agriculture. Both the Canaanites and the Hebrews at that time held the same essential religious belief. It was called territorial henotheism. This simply means that they believed in many gods, but that each god (or baal) was supreme in his own territory. As the various Hebrew tribes settled in Canaan they were tempted to abandon the worship of Yahweh, who was a mobile war god, and worship the baals who controlled the fertility of the area in which they had settled. This problem remained a live issue from 1200 B. C. to the time of the Babylonian exile (586 B. C.). It was a major theme of the prophets and the Deuteronomist (621 B. C.). The fact that some Hebrews did worship the baals is found in the fact that judges and leaders in Israel incorporated the word "baal" into their names. For example Gideon (a famous judge) originally was named "Jerubbaal" (let baal contend). King Saul's son was originally named Mephibaal. This name was changed by a later author to Mephibosheth (the Hebrew word for "shame" is *bosheth).*

Other problems were raised by the migration into Canaan which required measures of adaptation to the new situation. For example, difficulties were created by military pressure applied to the Hebrews by surrounding nations. The tribe of Benjamin was forced to pay tribute of oil, wine and wool to the Moabites for eighteen years until Ehud slew the Moabites' king, Eglon. Sisera lead the Canaanites in the north against the Hebrew leaders Deborah and Barak (Judges 5). Gideon was attacked by the Midianites in the southeast. Jepthath was opposed by the Ammonites, and Samson by the Philistines. This constant pressure from all sides would have had various effects upon the Hebrew tribes in Palestine. It forced them to unite so that they could overcome their enemies. It reinforced the worship of Yahweh to the exclusion of the baals since there was a need of a war god, and the Covenant demanded worship of him alone. In order to nullify this military pressure, the Hebrews were forced to learn the tactics and create weapons of defense.

E. The Political Problem

The change from a nomadic to a settled existence led to a change in the manner of government. The government of the nomadic clans by judges or chieftains was democratic to the extent that he in whom the Spirit of Yahweh was strong was chosen as the leader. A man's social position had nothing to do with the choice. The city-centered autocracy led to the establishment of dynasties. For example one strong man (Abimelech) ruled the City of Shechem instead of his 70 brothers.[5]

F. The Occupational Problem

The change from nomad to farmer or city dweller meant

that basic skills, customs, values, and habits had to be abandoned and new ones learned. Tent dwellers moved into and around walled towns. More implements (hardware) and new skills, such as stonecutting and metalworking had to be mastered. Even the basic dict changed from dairy products and meat to bread, vegetables, wine, and oil.

All these changes tended to disrupt and delay the coalescence into a nation of those Hebrew tribes who worshipped Yahweh. And yet, without the stability that such a culture offered, the nation would never have been able to emerge.

[1]Read Judges 17:1, 5, 7-13; 18:1-9, 11-29.

[2]This means that whatever takes place between the gods will be repeated in the world of nature, and *vice versa.*

[3]Other examples are Moses at the burning bush and the pillar of fire during the Exodus.

[4]Cf. *Christian Doctrine* by J. S. Whale, Cambridge University Press, 1950, page 82 ff., and Exodus 29.

[5]Cf. Judges 9:2.

Chapter XI

INFLUENCE OF "D".
THE BOOK OF SAMUEL

A. Three Deuteronomic Fictions

The writings of the Deuteronomic School, (D), are confined to the Book of Deuteronomy. However, authors who were interested in the power and control of the priestly cast are responsible for three fictitious Deuteronomic ideas which have infiltrated parts of the Bible written both before, and after, Deuteronomy. The three inaccurate ideas, or "fictions," are as follows:

1. There was only one ark, namely the Ark of the Covenant.

"Arks" were small chests or boxes that were a normal part of every Hebrew priest's equipment. They contained colored or inscribed stones or sticks, (terraphim), which when drawn out of the box at random gave a "yes" or "no" answer to a question asked of Yahweh through the priest. They represented the answer which coincided with Yahweh's will.[1] There were virtually as many arks as there were priests. Their use was the legal means of determining the will of Yahweh until the time of the prophets in the 8th century B. C. Small arks were probably carried on the priest's back like a knapsack; larger ones would be carried by two priests, suspended from poles supported on their shoulders. Some arks were more or less permanently located at the more important local shrines (e. g. the house of Micah, Shiloh, Dan, Bethel, etc.).

However, the view is almost uniformly expressed throughout the Bible that there was only one ark, namely the Ark of the Covenant, or the Ark of God. It is pictured as the rallying point for all Israel.[2] It had been kept at Shiloh and eventually was brought to Jerusalem by David and installed in the Temple by Solomon in the 10th century B. C. The Deuteronomic authors not only introduced the fiction that The Ark of the Covenant was unique, but even claimed that its orgin went back to the Exodus (cf. Deut. 31:25). It was supposed to contain the tablets of the Law received by Moses from Yahweh on Mt. Sinai.[3]

The purpose of this deception was to increase the prestige of Jerusalem as a center of priestly power. Jerusalem was actually not a vitally important city for the Hebrews until c. 800 B. C.

The means by which the editors were able to obscure the fact that there were many arks in Israel is very subtle. It is based on the fact that the two words translated as "ephod" and "ark" look very similar in Hebrew.

Ephod= אפוד
Ark= ארון

An ephod is a ceremonial apron-like garment worn by a priest. An ark is an oracle box as described above. When a Deuteronomist copied the Scripture or revised or annotated it, he changed the word "ark" into "ephod" by adding three small pen strokes and erasing the part of the "ן" that falls below the line. Two legitimate uses of the word are found in 1 Sam. 2:18 and 2 Sam. 6:14. It has been changed in many places. Three examples are: Judges 8:27, 1 Sam. 23:6, 1 Sam. 23:9.

2. The second fiction is the claim that there was only one legitimate place of worship, namely, Jerusalem.

This idea was perpetuated for the same reason as the first, to lend status to Jerusalem, the Temple, the priesthood, and the Law. The "D" authors were interested in protecting these institutions from contamination by the religious ideas of the surrounding nations. The statement of this second claim is found in Deuteronomy 12:2 ff. (Note that this was written in 621 B. C. but is supposed to refer to the period of Judges).

"You shall surely destroy all the places where

> the nations whom you shall dispossess served their gods, upon the high mountains and upon the hills and under every green tree; you shall tear down their altars, and dash in pieces their pillars, and burn their Asherim with fire; you shall hew down the images of their gods, and destroy their name out of that place. You shall not do so to the Lord your God. But you shall seek the place which the Lord your God will choose out of all your tribes to put his name and make his habitation there; thither you shall go, and thither you shall bring your burnt offerings and your sacrifices, your tithes and the offering you present, your votive offerings, your freewill offerings, and the firstlings of your herd and of your flock; and there you shall eat before the Lord your God, and you shall rejoice, you and your households, in all that you undertake, in which the Lord your God has blessed you."

Actually there were many legal places of worship until Deuteronomy was written (621 B. C.) and religious activity was indeed centered in Jerusalem. The Priestly School, however, carried the idea of Temple-type worship back to Moses with their elaborate and detailed description of the Tabernacle which was described as a movable Temple in use immediately after the Exodus (cf. Exodus 25).

There are Biblical references which indicate that worship and sacrifice were not only allowed but even encouraged in places besides Jerusalem. For example, Exodus 20:24:

> "An altar of earth you shall make for me and sacrifice on it your burnt offerings and your peace offerings, your sheep and your oxen; in every place where I cause my name to be remembered I will come to you and bless you."

Other examples are, Gideon's building an altar to the Lord at

Ophrah (Judges 6:24-26). When Saul first met Samuel, Samuel was sacrificing at a high place (1 Sam. 9:14). Solomon, (who built the all-important Temple where, according to D, all sacrifice must take place, used to offer 1000 burnt sacrifices at Gibeon (1 Kings 3:4). The prophet Elijah sacrificed on Mt. Carmel (1 Kings 18:20). When Jeroboam I (the first king of Israel) repaired the altars at Dan and Bethel he was merely doing the right and normal thing for his time, although the author of I Kings condemned him for it.

3. The third fiction is that there was only one legitimate priesthood, the Levitical.

The Deuteronomist in a further attempt to consolidate the power of the priesthood in the Temple at Jerusalem, restricted priests to members of the House of Levi.[4] The author states,

> " . . . and coming to the Levitical priests, and
> to the judge who is in office in those days,
> you shall consult them." (Deut. 17:9)

P is even more strict than this and limits the priesthood to those who can trace their lineage to Moses' brother Aaron. In this writing, the Levites become a subservient order.

The historical facts do not bear out these contentions, however. In the earliest days of the formation of the commonwealth (c. 1200 B. C.), and before, every man was his own priest. The head of the family sacrificed for those over whom he presided. The King sacrificed for the nation. David's sons were priests, yet they were from the tribe of Judah (2 Sam. 8:18). The true situation is described in the story of Micah and the Danites as discussed in the previous chapter.

B. The Books of Samuel

Just as the Pentateuch is the result of the editing of four authors – J, E, D, and P, so there are four literary sources of I and II Samuel. They are as follows:

1. The Old Source (sometimes called the Early Source or the Saul Source). This was probably the account of an eye-witness to the events that occurred in the middle of the 10th century B. C., principally the story of David. This author was in favor of the establishment of a monarchy by the Hebrews.
2. A Second Source (sometimes called the Late Source or

the Samuel Source) dates between 750 and 650 B. C. This writer is more dogmatic than the author of the Old Source. His view is that the future is determined by the conduct of the Israelites. He shows his disapproval of the establishment of a monarchy in Israel probably because he was afraid that contact with other monarchies would contaminate Israel.

3. There is some Deuteronomic material dating from c. 550 B. C.
4. Parts of the book were written after the Exile had ended (500-400 B. C.). These parts are 2 Sam. 7; 1 Sam. 2:1-10; and 2 Sam. 23:1-7.

B. Samuel and Saul

Let us assume the following chronology for Saul, David, and Solomon;

Saul: 1020-1000 B. C.
David: 1000-960 B. C.
Solomon: 960-922 B. C.

Since Samuel was a contemporary of Saul we may say that he flourished near the middle of the 11th century B. C. The Saul Source and the Samuel Source disagree on the details of the lives of Saul and Samuel and the relationship between the two men. The Saul Source describes Saul's rise to power and its approval by Yahweh through Samuel as follows:

Saul was looking for the lost asses of his father Kish. In the process of looking he came to the town where Samuel lived. Samuel was a seer, that is to say a man who had the gift of prophecy because of the Ruach[5] of Yahweh with which he was filled. Samuel told Saul that the asses had been found, and then secretly annointed Saul as the man Yahweh had chosen to be a prince or ruler over all of Israel. On the way home the Spirit of Yahweh "came mightily" upon Saul. He too was given the gift of prophecy and he was "turned into another man" (1 Sam. 10:6).

Saul's recognition as ruler by the other Hebrew tribes came about as the result of the siege of the Israelite city of Jabesh in Gilead, by Nahash, leader of the hostile Ammonites. Nahash promised to lift the seige if the men of Jabesh would allow him to gouge out their right eyes. The elders of the city arranged for a week of truce while they sought a solution. When Saul heard of their predicament he cut up a yoke of oxen, sending pieces to all the Hebrew tribes, threatening them with similar dismemberment if they did not follow him in war against the Ammonites. The call was heeded, the Ammonites defeated, and Jabesh-Gilead delivered. After this heroic act, all the Hebrews accepted Saul as their king in a ceremony in Gilgal. The steadfastness of the loyalty of the men of Jabesh-Gilead is seen in the fact that they rescued his body from the Philistines by storming the walls of Beth Shan after Saul was slain by the Philistines many years later.

The later Samuel Source gives a different account of Samuel and Saul. In this account Samuel is a judge, not a seer. His judgeship led to triumphs over the Philistines (cf. 1 Sam. 7:5-14). The author clearly indicates that the idea of a monarchy is displeasing to Yahweh, but the tribes insisted, and Samuel begrudgingly gave in with the warning that a king would limit their freedom and subject them to a despotic tyrrany. He chose Saul as the leader, and Saul was annointed before all the people at Mizpah (not Gilgal).

It should be kept in mind that the Saul Source was written after the disastrous collapse of the monarchy under Solomon which may account for the feeling that a monarchy is not a guarantee for stability. It is also possible that the author believed there was only one true king, namely Yahweh. Furthermore, the experiment with a unified government at Shechem under the leadership of Abimelech had proved a failure.[6]

In any event, Samuel played an important part in the change which occurred from a loose tribal confederacy as described in Judges to the full-fledged monarchies of David and Solomon. Samuel was a prophet-judge involved in the formation of an intermediary pre-monarchic confederacy under the leadership of Saul. As a prophet-judge he was a man through whom the will of Yahweh might be made known. Apparently he also had some part in breaking the grip of the Philistines on the Hebrews.

C. King Saul

Saul was a tragic figure in the history of Israel. He was rejected by Samuel who represented the old order, and was overshadowed by David who represented a new way of life. Samuel's rejection came to a climax when Saul, after defeating the Amalekites, did not completely carry out the sacrificial ban (herem).[7] He spared the life of Agag, king of Amalek, and the best of the Amalekite cattle. Samuel hewed Agag to pieces himself.

> "Then Samuel went to Ramah; and Saul went up to his house in Gibeah of Saul. And Samuel did not see Saul again until the day of his death, but Samuel grieved over Saul. And the Lord repented that he had made Saul king over Israel." (1 Sam. 15:35)

The Spirit of Yahweh increased in David as it diminished in Saul. David's popularity grew as a result of his military successes over the Philistines, until finally the women were singing in the streets.

"Saul has slain his thousands and David his ten thousands". (1 Sam. 18:7)

Saul was increasingly handicapped by a mental illness which manifested itself in fits of depression and delusions of persecution. Finally Samuel anointed David king in place of Saul (1 Sam. 16:13).

The biography of Saul is not an unbiased one, however. There are three reasons for this:

1. The Early, or Saul Source, is an account from the south (Judah), whereas Saul was a northerner from the tribe of Benjamin.
2. The purpose of both the Saul and Samuel Sources was to build up David at the expense of Saul.
3. The first three chapters of 1 Samuel, plus the Deuteronomic material, had a priestly origin. Saul was unpopular with the priests because:
   a. He refused to carry out herem against the Amalekites.
   b. Saul ordered 85 priests put to death at Nob because they helped David escape (1 Sam. 22).
   c. He summoned the priest Ahijah to obtain a divine oracle, but abruptly ended the consultation when the military situation indicated that there was no time to wait for Yahweh's answer (1 Sam. 14:18-23).
   d. When his hungry soldiers slaughtered cattle they ate meat with the blood still in it (i. e. against ritual procedure). He also built an altar for sacrifice himself (1 Sam. 14:31-35).

In spite of these criticisms Saul was an important king. There are many indications that he was a great man. They are as follows:

a. He united the tribes of Israel sufficiently well to defeat Nahash the Ammonite.

b. He was the first strong Israelite king.
c. He was able to hold off the Philistines and actually defeated them at Michmash (1 Sam. 14).
d. He ruled not only in the north, but also some people in the south.
e. He won favor east of the Jordan River (viz. Jabesh Gilead).
f. He had an army but raised no taxes.
g. He was popular – there was never a revolt against him.

[1] The words *Urim* and *Thummim* often occur in conjunction with descriptions of the use of arks, but the meaning of these words is not clear.

[2] Cf. 1 Sam. 4

[3] These tablets would correspond to the terraphim.

[4] Levi was one of the sons of Jacob and Leah

[5] Note that the "Ruach" and the "Spirit" of Yahweh mean the same. Cf. pp. 75-76.

[6] Cf. Judges 9.

[7] Cf. 1 Sam. 15.

Chapter XII

THE MONARCHY UNDER DAVID AND SOLOMON

A. *The Rise of David to Power*

In his personal life David advanced from a shepherd to a king. Simultaneously he led the national growth of the Hebrews from a rustic monarchy under Saul to a nation of significant size. His biography is found in those parts of 1 Samuel which come from the Early Source, and in 2 Samuel, which is nearly all written by the author of the Early Source except for some editorial comments.

His character was formed from a strange mixture of kindness and cruelty, of strengths and weaknesses. He became a member of Saul's court when he was a youth. The Early Source relates that he was brought into Saul's household in order to play the lyre during the king's fits of depression. The Late Source claims that David was brought to Saul's attention when he killed Goliath. However, the Early Source attributes the slaying of Goliath to a contemporary hero of the Hebrews named Elhanan (cf. 2 Sam. 21:19: 1 Chron. 20:5; 2 Sam. 23:24; 1 Chron. 11:26). It is probable that Elhanan was the real giant killer, but the story was told in connection with David in order to increase his reputation.

At first David found favor with Saul. He became a life-long

friend of Saul's son Jonathan and he married Michal, Saul's daughter. This initial favor soon turned into animosity partly because of the nature of Saul's mental illness (perhaps paranoia), and partly because of jealously. David was forced to flee for his life, stopping at Nob where the priest Ahimelech fed him and armed him with Goliath's sword. This act was classified as treachery by Saul who extracted his revenge by slaying Ahimelech and eighty-five priests who served at the altar at Nob.

David escaped to the cave of Adullam in the hill country of Judah where he became the ring leader of about 400 malcontents. From there he and his band of brigands moved about the desert. His dealings with Nabal and his wife Abigail (1 Sam. 25) show the crueler side of his nature – this instance was one of blackmail. Finally David allied himself with Achish, king of the Philistine city of Gath. Achish allowed David and his band to settle in the city of Ziklag, near the border of Philistia and Judah. From this headquarters, David raided, despoiled, and demolished settlements which were hostile to the Hebrews, but he told Achish that the spoils came from encounters with his own people, the Israelites. Although Achish was taken in by this strategy, the other Philistine kings did not trust David, and rejected his offer to help against Saul.

While David and his men had gone to Aphek in anticipation of joining forces with the Philistines against Saul, the Amalekites overran Ziklag, burned it and took the women, children, and cattle as plunder. Upon returning to Ziklag, David overtook the Amalekites, defeated them, freed the captives, and divided the spoil among the elders in Judah. In this way he gained favor in the South. When Saul was defeated and killed by the Philistines on Mt. Gilboa, David was anointed king of Judah at Hebron. He was 30 years old, and ruled over Judah for 7½ years.

Saul's leadership over northern Palestine fell to his son, Ishbosheth (Ishbaal). He was a weak man, and Abner the leader of his army defected, turning the northern tribes over to David. At the age of 37, David was anointed King over all of Israel at Hebron (2 Sam. 5:3). He confirmed and entrenched his position of power by capturing Jerusalem and establishing his capitol there. Since Jerusalem is in the center of Palestine, the northern and southern tribes were united geographically. By bringing the Ark of the Covenant to Jerusalem, the old traditions and the new city were joined by means of a continuous religious custom. He fought successfully against the Moabites, the Syrians, the Ammonites, the Edomites, the Amalekites and the Philistines. These victories, plus a treaty with Hiram, king of Tyre, brought a measure of stability to the times. David instituted the structure of a small empire in that there was an administration of the law by the king (2 Sam. 14:4-17), he had a recorder, a secretary, a harem, a priest, a census, a tax system, an organization of forced labor, and a personally controlled corps of soldiers.

B. David's Character

David's biography shows him to be a man in whom strengths and weaknesses exist in remarkable contrast. Each one must make his own assessment of David's character. However, it is apparent that the author of the Early Source in Samuel was biased in favor of the king. Following is a comparison of David's strengths and weaknesses:

1. David's Strengths:
   a. He was a brilliant military commander with great personal courage.
   b. He was a gifted organizer.
   c. He was a shrewd politician. He bewailed the death of Saul and of Abner, Saul's general, and of Ishbaal, Saul's son, hence placating his potential enemies in the house of Saul. After Saul's death he restored Michal, Saul's daughter, to his court, thus consolidating his ties with the northern tribes. His choice of Jerusalem as his capitol was a sound tactic, as was his retention of the ark and the priesthood. His gift of Amalekite spoils to the elders of Judah enhanced his popularity in the south. All these acts required foresight and imagination and were directed to maintaining stability and unity between the northern and the southern tribes.
   d. He was a talented poet and musician (cf. David's lament, 2 Sam. 1:19 ff.).
   e. He was generous. He shared the spoils at Ziklag and cared for Mephibosheth, Saul's lame son (2 Sam. 9). He did not kill Saul when Saul, his enemy, was in his power.
   f. His capacity for deep friendship is seen in his relationship with Jonathan.
2. David's Weaknesses:

a. He committed many immoral acts. He blackmailed Nabal, committed adultery with Bathsheba, treacherously murdered Bathsheba's husband Uriah, killed the messengers that brought news of the deaths of Saul, Abner, and Ishbaal, he lied to Achish, and treated Michal cruelly in taking her away from her husband Paltiel.
b. He was not able to control Joab, the commander of his army. Joab killed Abner, the commander of Saul's army, and Absalom, David's son, against the orders of the king. Joab also killed Amasa after David had appointed him head of his army. (2 Sam. 20:4 ff.)
c. He was not able to control his own family. Absalom was spoiled and a dangerous enemy.
d. He was unpopular because of his taxes and forced labor. There were two major revolts against him, Sheba's and Absalom's.
e. Although he succeeded in transferring the traditions of the confederacy (ark and priesthood) to Jerusalem, Israel was no longer the people of God bound together on the basis of a covenant allegiance to Yahweh at the central sanctuary. The bond became a political one between the citizens of a state.

In spite of these changes in the nature of social organization of the Hebrews, later generations looked back on David's reign as the golden age of Israel. Its emblem became the star of David and its focal point the city of David. Even the Messiah was expected to arise from the direct lineal descendency of David.

C. The Sources of the Book of Kings.

The two books of Kings were originally one book. Its contents and purpose are not historical in an objective sense. It was written to save Judah by pointing out that Israel, the northern kingdom, fell because of its moral laxness.[1] The theme of 1 and 2 Kings is Deuteronomic, namely that faithfulness to Yahweh leads to his blessing, and a neglect of the covenant leads to disaster. The material in these books is highly selective in favor of the southern kingdom.

The literary sources of the two books of kings can be diagrammed as follows:

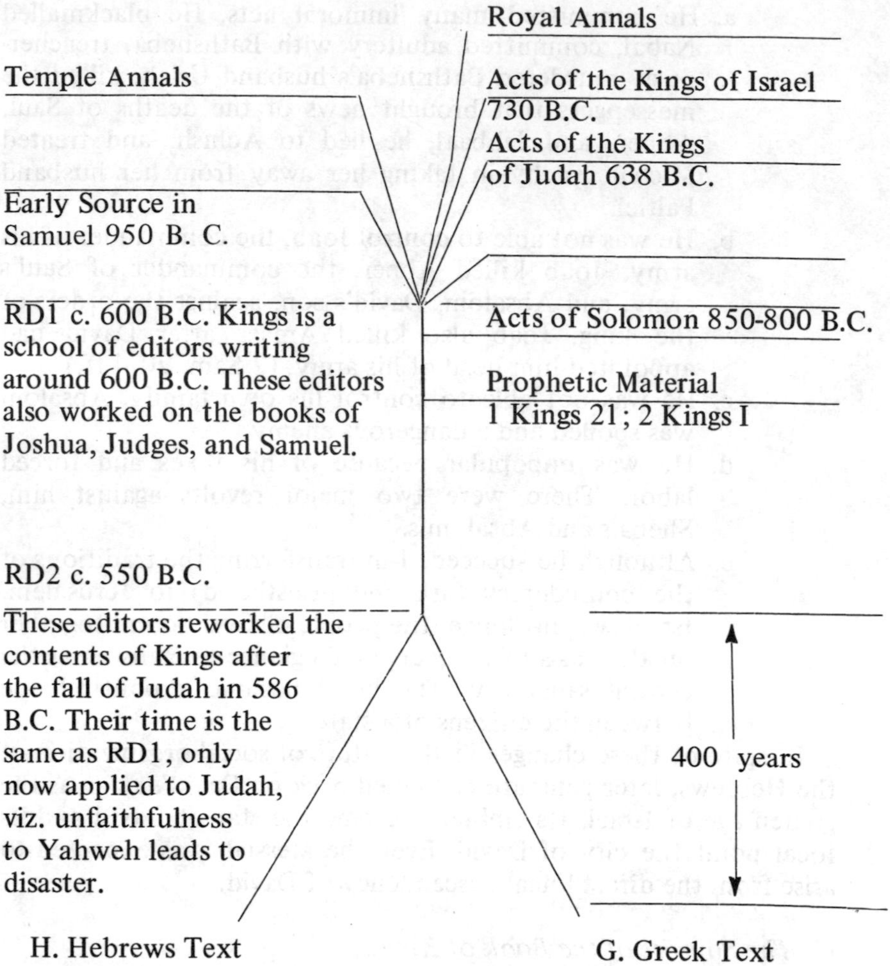
Royal Annals
Temple Annals
Acts of the Kings of Israel
730 B.C.
Acts of the Kings
of Judah 638 B.C.
Early Source in
Samuel 950 B. C.
RD1 c. 600 B.C. Kings is a
school of editors writing
around 600 B.C. These editors
also worked on the books of
Joshua, Judges, and Samuel.
Acts of Solomon 850-800 B.C.
Prophetic Material
1 Kings 21; 2 Kings I
RD2 c. 550 B.C.
These editors reworked the
contents of Kings after
the fall of Judah in 586
B.C. Their time is the
same as RD1, only
now applied to Judah,
viz. unfaithfulness
to Yahweh leads to
disaster.
400 years
H. Hebrews Text
G. Greek Text

D. King Solomon

The story of Solomon's reign is found in 1 Kings. It is a short and uncomplicated narrative. Under the leadership of Solomon, Israel grew into a small but prosperous empire. It was large enough, nevertheless, to win the respect and envy of the Queen of Sheba and the King of Tyre. However, this growth took place at the cost of the liberty of the Israelites. Solomon's oppressive measures lead to a revolt after this death which in turn divided the kingdom into autonomous governments in the north

(Israel) and the south (Judah). It should be kept in mind in reading Kings that Solomon's historian has been generous out of respect for the sanctity of the Davidic lineage. The true picture emerges when one reads between the lines. Solomon's good points were as follows:

1. He had a reputation as an author of proverbs, as a scientific scholar, and as an efficient administrator.
2. He was noted for his wisdom, and even in our day this survives as the well known phrase "the wisdom of Solomon."
3. He built the Temple in Jerusalem which became (and to a certain extent still is) a focal point for worship in Judaism.

Just as David had his weaknesses, so did Solomon. They may be listed as follows:

1. His reign was one of outward splendor but internal decay.
2. He instituted the use of forced labor from among captured enemies as well as his own countrymen.
3. He established a method of taxation which replaced the twelve tribes with twelve tax districts. The boundaries of the districts were established in such a way that tribal unity was weakened. The loss of tribal identification also impaired the idea of national unity – a nation formed of the twelve tribes of Israel.
4. The economic measures he took to maintain himself in luxury led to the downfall of the kingdom in the next generation. He was forced to sell Israelite cities to keep his court going (1 Kings 9:10-14).
5. It took 13 years to build his own house as opposed to 7 years to build the Temple. This is a guide to the ratio of self interest to national interest.
6. His many foreign wives and concubines were allowed (and assisted) to maintain the practice of worshipping their own gods. Such an example at the highest level of leadership undercut the vital principle of the covenant.

[1]The monarchy split in 933 B.C. after the death of Solomon. The northern tribes became the Kingdom of Israel and the southern tribes the Kingdom of Judah. Israel was exterminated in 721 B.C. by the Assyrians.

Chapter XIII

THE DIVIDED MONARCHY.
JUDAH (922 B. C. – 586 B. C.).
ISRAEL (922 B. C. – 721 B. C.).

A. The Division.

After Solomon's death, his son Rehoboam was to take the throne following the established custom. However, due to his disregard of the advice of the elders and his threat to continue his father's oppressive measures of forced labor and taxation, the 10 northern tribes rejected Rehoboam and established an independent monarchy with its capital at Shechem. Jerusalem was retained as the capital of the southern kingdom of Judah. There were five important kings of the northern kingdom of Israel: Jeroboam I, Omri, Ahab, Jehu, and Jeroboam II.

B. The Kings of Israel.

1. Jeroboam I (922-901 B. C.).[1] The biography of Jeroboam I (as well as those of the other four kings of Israel) came from the south. Therefore, they are biased and tend to be uncomplimentary. One of Jeroboam's first acts was to establish sanctuaries at Dan in the north and Bethel in the south, to replace Jerusalem as a place of worship. At

each of these sanctuaries, golden calves were set up. The author accuses Jeroboam of worshipping the calves (perhaps a reference to the worship of the golden calf by the Hebrews under the leadership of Aaron while Moses was on Sinai receiving the tablets of the Law). However, there is also evidence that the calves served as a kind of golden throne for Yahweh who continued to be worshipped as the god of the Israelites.

2. Omri (880-869 B. C.). Omri was a second King David. He first built Tirzah and then Samaria as his capitals, in a way reminiscent of David's building Jerusalem. He is mentioned as an important king by the prophet Micah (Micah 6:16), in the Syrian annals, and on the Moabite Stone. Mesha, King of Moab wrote, "Moab was long oppressed by Omri, King of Israel." Heavy annual tribute was paid by Moab to Israel (2 Kings 3:4). Not much is said about him in Kings, but he was a great king.
3. Ahab (869-850 B. C.). Ahab, Omri's son, was a second Solomon just as Omri was a second David. Shalmanezer III, king of Assyria (858-824 B. C.), records a battle against a coalition of Near Eastern kings in which were 10,000 foot soldiers and 2,000 chariots contributed by Ahab. Ahab also controlled Bashan and Gilead east of the Jordan. He married Jezebel, Queen of Tyre, and thus reintroduced baal worship to the Israelites. He was confronted by the prophet Elijah.
4. Jehu (842-815 B. C.). Jehu ascended the throne as the result of an army revolt which killed King Joran of Omri's dynasty. Jezebel was also killed at this time. The Black Obelisk of Shalmanezer III depicts Jehu paying tribute to the Assyrian king.[2]
5. Jeroboam II (786-746 B. C.). This fifth and last important king of Israel expanded the boundaries of the northern kingdom until they extended from Hamath to the Arabah (See Map 5 in the Oxford Annotated Bible).

C. Elijah the Tishbite.

The story of the prophet Elijah is found in chapters 17, 18, 19, and 21 of 1 Kings. It is from a special source which is free from Deuteronomic influence (for example it is permissible to build an altar on Mt. Carmel far to the north of Jerusalem). Elijah was a prophet, that is, a man in whom the spirit of Yahweh was found.

The story of the contest on Mount Carmel (1 Kings 18:20-40) climaxes the struggles between the baals and Yahweh on the baals' home ground. An altar was built, and the baals and Yahweh were called to descend upon it. Before calling on the name of Yahweh, Elijah[3] poured four jars of water on the altar three times. This was an act intended to create sympathetic magic. As Elijah poured the water, so would Yahweh pour water on the land. Four jars three times = 12 jars of water. This has some special significance to the Hebrews. Three and four were complete numbers, cf. also the 12 original tribes of Hebrews.

There are other less significant references to the power of Yahweh. When Elijah stayed with the widow of Zarephath (a Phoenician city), he was supported by means of a miraculous meal jar and oil cruse that were always full. The prophet even held power over life and death as seen in his restoration of the widow's son to life. This element of magic and miracle is present in many of the stories about Elijah, even to the end of his life, where he did not die but was received into heaven by means of a chariot and horses of fire in a whirlwind (double symbolism for the presence of Yahweh). These details, of course, must not be taken literally, but symbolically and mythologically. They may have been introduced in part to increase the stature of Elijah, but basically they are saying that Yahweh is the ultimate controller of all things that happen *in every part* of the earth.

D. Retreat to Sinai.

Elijah's slaughter of Jezebel's 450 prophets of Baal stirred up the wrath of the queen who swore vengeance by means of the prophet's death. Elijah fled south to the Mountain of God (Mt. Sinai or Mt. Horeb). The account of his journey and encounter with God (1 Kings 19) is an attempt to describe the change which occurred in the Hebrew's understanding of the nature of Yahweh. There is an implicit comparison with the first encounter between Yahweh and the Israelites through his confrontation with Moses. At that time Yahweh was envisioned as a storm god whose presence was manifested in wind, lighting, fire, and earthquake (cf. Exodus 19). Just as Moses withdrew from the awe-full presence of Yahweh by hiding in a cleft in the rock, so did Elijah (cf. Exodus 33:18-34:8).

The story of Elijah's encounter with Yahweh reveals a new and deeper understanding of the nature of God. He is more than the powerful life-giving god of the wind or breath or whirlwind (Ruach). He is more than the destroyer, transformer god of fire. He is more than the all-powerful earth-shaker god of the earthquake. He is found more clearly in the "still small voice," in a man's conscience, within the deepest and innermost resources of every man.

[1] The chronology of the kings of Israel is far from certain. The figures given are those of W. F. Albright. Other chronologies differ with variations of about 10 years, not unusual.

[2] Jehoahaz (815-801 B. C.) succeeded Jehu. He ruled during the lowest ebb of Israel's fortune.

[3] The name Elijah in Hebrew means "(My) God is Yah (weh)."

Chapter XIV

The Concept of Messiah

A. Definition of Terms.

The word "messiah" comes from the Hebrew word meaning "to anoint." Anything or anyone within Judaism that was anointed was thereby filled with the holiness of Yahweh, and was set aside for a special purpose. We must distinguish between The Messiah and messiah-figures. By The Messiah we shall mean Yahweh's special agent or judge who would establish a new world order on the Last Day, or the Day of Judgment as the Hebrews expected it. The Messiah is a specific semi-divine person. Messiah figures are found in every culture outside as well as inside Judaism. They are those men (usually kings, or judges, or priests) that stand between man and God, and whose function it is to guard the continuance of a right relationship between man and God. They are usually considered to be semi-divine, such as the pharaoh in Egypt, the legendary heroes of Greece, Babylonian kings, the Roman emperors, and even the Emperor of Japan until the end of World War II.

B. The Idea of a Messiah in Judaism.

An investigation of the history of the concept of Messiah

shows three things quite clearly, viz.: 1. The extreme complexity of the concept which is due in part to the universality of the idea, 2. A wide divergence of opinion among scholars about broad aspects of messianism as well as disagreement about details, 3. An extreme paucity of literature bearing on the subject.

The best treatment of the historical background is W.O.E. Oesterley's treatise published in 1908 under the title *The Evolution of the Messianic Idea.* He defines the scope of the title as "The method whereby the conception of a Savior, overcoming all that is harmful to man and bringing about for man a state of peacefulness, became gradually more and more understood and apprehended by men."

Oesterley has postulated three basic mythological ideas which have developed within the consciousness of primeval man and which therefore have arisen more or less simultaneously within widely separated cultures. Since these myths were based on man's basic emotions, and the emotions are universal, there is a close similarity in the myths. The three basic emotions are fear, a sense of dependence, and the desire to be happy. The emotion of fear developed by starvation, storm, cold, wild animals, drought, and disease. The fact that nature was constantly in opposition to man coupled with an animistic outlook gave rise to the belief that all nature was inhabited by a malignant spirit. This primeval cruel monster was identified with evil. It was also thought to have had a creative function. Its home was in the sea and it became identified with the deep. This myth Oesterley calls the Tehom-myth from Genesis 1:2, "The earth was waste and void, and darkness was on the face of the Tehom." This idea of evil being incarnate in a serpent, a sea-monster, Leviathan, a dragon, the sea is scattered throughout the Old Testament. A typical passage is Isaiah 27:1, "In that day shall Yahweh punish with his terrible, mighty, and powerful sword Leviathan the coiling serpent, Leviathan the crooked serpent; yea he will slay the dragon that is in the sea." Other examples are: Amos 9:3, Isaiah 30:7, (Rahab is a synonym for Tehom), Psalm 74:12-15, Psalm 89:9-11, and Job 26:12-13.

An identical myth appears in Chaldean, Phoenician, Egyptian, Zoroastrian, Greek, Algonquin, Iroquois, South American, Mexican, African, and Peruvian culture – to name only part.

The second basic emotion, a sense of dependence, was the natural outcome of primitive man's position as he lived at the mercy of the forces of nature. The feeling was heightened by the fact that he felt all parts of nature were indwelt by spirits with which he was unable to cope. The fact that nature was hostile or indifferent led to a search for help in overcoming this environment. The search led to a second myth – that of the Savior-Hero or Heilbringer. The Yahweh-myth was the Hebrew adaptation of this universal theme.

The early Jew did not have a doctrine of creation *ex-nihilo*. Tehom, the watery darkness, was existent first. Then Yahweh the Savior-Hero came and created man and what he needed out of the chaos. The Heilbringer overcame the primeval watery monster and brought temporal blessings to the people. Biblical examples that support this point are found in Genesis 2:6-19, Psalm 65: 7,8 (6,7), Psalm 74:12-17, Psalm 89:6-19. A similar myth is also found in the early literature of the Babylonian, Egyptian, Indian, Zoroastrian, Greek, Algonquin, Zulu, and Maya cultures and many others.

Lastly, the universal longing for happiness led to the Paradise-myth. Man's ancient desire for happiness led to fantasies concerning a blessed state. The fantasies became fixed and embedded in tradition. There was ease, comfort, freedom from pain, and universal peace which even the animals shared. A longing for a return of this golden age would naturally lead to a projected hope for its future return under the leadership of a divine ruler whose power stemmed from the Savior-Hero. The hope for a return gradually hardened into a fixed expectation.

The myth appeared in the Hebrew Bible. The perfect time past was the Garden of Eden. The hope for a return of a time of peace and prosperity is widespread throughout the prophet writings. "And it shall come to pass in the latter days that the mountain of Yahweh's house shall be established on the top of the mountains and shall be exalted above the hills; and all nations shall flow into it." (Isaiah 2:2). Other typical examples are Psalm 48:2-4, Ezekiel 28:13-15, Isaiah 11:1-10, Isaiah 35:1-10. The paradise myth is also found in the literature of all other major cultures.

These three basic myths of mankind when taken together form a logical structure. In the beginning was the water monster, Tehom, evil and powerful. But man cannot believe in an evil power alone. The Savior-Hero came and fought with the serpent giving man good gifts. But man yearns for the time when the Heilbringer's victory will be complete. He looks back to a time of perfection that existed in God's garden, and he looks forward to a time when Leviathan will be killed and nature and man will be at peace. "And I saw a new heaven and a new earth; for the first heaven and the first earth are passed away; *and the Sea is no more."* (Rev. 21:1).

These are the three basic myths that permeated the thinking of all mankind. Their Hebrew forms were the Tehom-myth, the Yahweh-myth, and the Paradise-myth. It was out of these three basic concepts that the Messianic idea came. It is so complex that it can no longer be traced definitively. It was developed in different forms, in different ages, by different people. One example of the development of the Messianic idea can be traced through the book of Isaiah. Four passages are involved as follows:

1. Isaiah 2:2-4.

> It shall come to pass in the latter days that the house of the Lord
> shall be established as the highest of the mountains, and shall be raised above the hills;
> and all nations shall flow to it, and many peoples shall come, and say:
> "Come, let us go up to the mountains of the Lord, to the house of the God of Jacob;
> that he may teach us his ways and that we may walk in his paths."
> For out of Zion shall go forth the law, and the word of Yahweh from Jerusalem.
> He shall judge between the nations, and shall decide for many peoples;
> and they shall beat their swords into plowshares, and their spears into pruning hooks;
> nation shall not lift up sword against nation, neither shall they learn war any more.

Here Yahweh is himself the Messianic ruler. His subjects are all the nations upon the earth.

2. Isaiah 4:2-6.

> In that day the branch of the Lord shall be beautiful and glorious, and the fruit of the land shall be the pride and glory of the survivors of Israel.

And he who is left in Zion and remains in Jerusalem will be called holy, every one who has been recorded for life in Jerusalem, when the Lord shall have washed away the filth of the daughters of Zion and cleansed the bloodstains of Jerusalem from its midst by a spirit of judgement and by a spirit of burning. Then the Lord will create over the whole site of Mount Zion and over her assemblies a cloud by day, and smoke and the shining of a flaming fire by night; for over all the glory there will be a canopy and a pavilion. It will be for shade by day from the heat, and for a refuge and a shelter from the storm and rain.

Here Yahweh is one step removed – his presence marked by smoke and fire. His subjects are only the purified children of Israel.

3. Isaiah 9:6,7.

For to us a child is born, to us a son is given; and the government will be upon his shoulder, and his name will be called
"Wonderful Counselor, Mighty God, Everlasting Father, Prince of Peace."
Of the increase of his government and of peace, there will be no end,
upon the throne of David, and over his kingdom, to establish it, and to uphold it with justice and with righteousness from this time forth and for evermore.
The zeal of the Lord of hosts will do this.

The Messiah is here a divine human ruler.

4. Isaiah 11:1-5.

There shall come forth a shoot from the stump of Jesse, and a branch shall grow out of his roots.
And the Spirit of the Lord shall rest upon him, and the spirit of wisdom and understanding, the spirit of counsel and might, the spirit of knowledge and the fear of the Lord. He shall not judge by what his eyes see, or decide

by what his ears hear;
but with righteousness he shall judge the poor, and decide with equity for the meek of the earth;
and he shall smite the earth with the rod of his mouth, and with the breath of his lips he shall slay the wicked.
Righteousness shall be the girdle of his waist, and faithfulness the girdle of his loins.

The Messiah is purely human. He is a descendant of Jesse and his subjects are restricted to the children of Israel.

As it has been shown, three basic primeval myths underlie the messianic idea. But in addition there is another strand of a more historical nature that was woven with the myths to further develop the idea. The word 'messiah' is the clue to the origin of this strand. It is derived from the Hebrew word Mashah (anointment). The custom of pouring oil over a holy stone as a libation was an ancient one in Israel. The custom of anointing was also common in an independent form among the Egyptians, Babylonians, and Canaanites during the earliest years of Israel's history (c. 1200). It acquired a sanctifying character when holy oil was used. Oil, like blood, developed independent importance as a holy object and it was used to consecrate kings (Judges 9:8, I Sam. 16:3-12, I Kings 1:34-39), prophets (I Kings 19:16, Isaiah 61:1), and priests (Ex. 28:41, Ex. 29:7,29,36, Ex. 30:30) as well as to sanctify implements of various kinds. The act of anointing became an act of consecration as well as a mark of institution. The king as God's Annointed (Messiah) partook of Yahweh's power and stood as a link between Yahweh and his people. The king became an intermediary through which Yahweh's gifts came. Here there is no eschatological dimension in the Messianic idea. The fulfillment during the monarchical period was considered to be in the present.

The Messianic literature that stems from this period is contained in the "enthronement psalms," or "royal psalms." These psalms were probably originally composed for use at religious celebrations such as coronations, royal marriages or perhaps the celebration of a New Year's festival commemorating Yahweh's ascension to his throne. The fact that it was the custom in Babylon and Assyria for kings to be coronated on the New Year's day following the death of their predecessors may have been reflected in Israel in the form of a New Year's celebration at the coronation of a king (see Jeremiah 26:1, 2; 27:1, and 28:1).

The New Year's celebration was a memorial of Yahweh's victory over the powers of chaos at the creation of the world. It is a repetition of the ancient theme of the Yahweh-myth and the Tehom-myth in a re-enactment of the battle of Yahweh with the serpent. Psalm 2 represents literature used prior to the ritual combat. Contemporary parallels from enthronement festivals of Assyria and Babylonia show a similar re-enactment in which the king appears as a penitent. His royal insignia are removed, he is boxed on the ears and has his beard pulled by a priest. A reflection of this may be found in the suffering servant songs in Isaiah (cf. Isaiah 42:1-4; 49:1-6; 50:4-9; 52:13-15;53).

In any event although the concept of the king as Yahweh's annointed may have served its purpose during the monarchy (especially under David), with the subsequent fall of Israel in 721 and Judah in 586 a new point of view developed. The prophets looked at the corruption to which the office of king had been subject. They looked back at the golden days of David's reign, and then predicted a future time of blessedness under a Messiah, an anointed – chosen by Yahweh from among the descendants of David.

This idea of a Messianic descendant of David appears in a vague precursive form as early as the J source in Genesis:

Genesis 49:10, 11.

> The scepter shall not depart from Judah, nor the ruler's staff from between his feet, until he comes to whom it belongs; and to him shall be the obedience of the peoples. Binding his foal to the vine and his ass's colt to the choice vine, he washes his garments in wine and his vesture in the blood of grapes.

However it becomes clear subsequent to the time of Jeremiah. (c. 600 B. C.) (See Jer. 23:5, 6; 33:15, 16, Ezekiel 34:23, 24; 37:24).

In conjunction with the idea of messianic rule is the concept of "The Day of the Lord." This concept must have been popular by the time of Amos (c. 750), since he denounces so strongly those who look for this day. Popular conception held that it was a joyful time – but the prophets saw it as a day when Yahweh would come and rule in righteousness, bringing judgment upon all men including the children of Israel.

This belief in the Day of the Lord or Golden Age was marked

by two points: 1. One of its chief characteristics was peace and 2. It was to be an age of happiness and contentment. These two characteristics were adopted into messianic literature in describing the age of the Messiah's rule. For the idea of peace see Isaiah 2:4 (sword into plowshares), 11:9 (They shall not hurt or destroy in all my holy mountain.) Isaiah 9:6 (the Prince of Peace), Jer. 23:5, 6, Ezekiel 34:22-25, Ezekiel 37:24-28, Isaiah 35:9, Zech, 9:9-10 (Rejoice greatly, O daughter of Zion). For examples of how messianic writing adopted the idea of happiness and contentment of the Day of the Lord see Isaiah 40:1-3; 25:6.

Messianic hope received a new complexion in the Apocalyptic writings from about 200 B. C. to the time of Christ. Apocalypicism was the outgrowth of prophecy. These writers continued the theme of "The Day of the Lord" after the age of prophets had past. The writing was subject to Hellenistic and Persian influences. The chief examples of apocalyptic writing are Daniel, Joel, Isaiah 24-27, Zech. 9-14, Ezekiel 38, 39, Obadiah, the Apocryphal book of II Esdras, and in the pseudepigrapha Jubilees, Testamonies of the Twelve Patriarchs, Enoch, and the Psalms of Solomon. In the New Testament the Book of Revelation contains much apocalyptic writing.

The common elements of eschatological messianism as found in apocalyptic literature are as follows:

1. Two ages, the present age and the age to come.
2. The belief that the present age is evil and under Satan's influence.
3. Belief that the good age to come will be introduced by God or his representative through a catastrophe.
4. There will be a final judgement (in some literature two judgements). The judge is either God or his Messiah.
5. The new kingdom of the Jews will be the kingdom of God. This kingdom is the great characteristic of the new age. (A variation is the establishment of a messianic kingdom of limited duration followed by God's permanent control over men).
6. The resurrection of the righteous.
7. A personal Messiah possibly foreshadowed by the coming of Elijah.

This was the progress of the idea – of a Messiah up to the time that Jesus appeared. One of the basic beliefs of Christianity from earliest times has been that Jesus was the Messiah. Almost every Messianic text was considered to be a direct prophecy bearing on his life regardless of the original context. Where did the idea of his messiahship originate? Jesus' own ideas on the subject? How did he consider himself?

Chapter XV

THE HEBREW CONCEPT OF SOUL. A REVIEW OF HISTORICAL EVENTS IN ISRAEL IN THE 8TH, 7TH, AND 6TH CENTURIES B. C.

A. Nephesh.

Nephesh is a transliteration of a Hebrew word which is usually translated into English as "soul." This is unfortunate because the English word "soul" conveys quite well what the Greeks meant by *pneuma* (also translated into English as "soul"), but there is no word in English that stands for the Hebrew concept of *nephesh.* For the Hebrew, *nephesh* is the chief component of life. In the act of creation Yahweh took the dust of the ground and by his breath *(ruach)* transformed it into a living *nephesh.* Such as he is, man in his total essence is a *nephesh.*[1] Each man, each *nephesh* has its peculiar and unique stamp that makes it identifiable. Hence a man's appearance, his voice, his way of acting, his odor, all that he has done (all his past acts), and even all of his possessions when taken together constitute the man's *nephesh* and stamp the essence of his being with its special characteristics.

For the Hebrew a man's will is not something apart, but is the tendency of the totality of the soul. It directs the *nephesh* along a certain course. Sometimes this will is referred to as "heart" (e. g. "the heart of Pharaoh was hardened").

Spirit[2] (either Yahweh's or man's) acts upon the soul and causes it; the way in which it goes is determined by the will. A crude analogy can be given by equating the soul *(nephesh)* with an automobile. It is what gets a man to his destination. The will is the steering wheel. It determines the direction in which the *nephesh* goes. The spirit *(ruach)* is like the engine, furnishing the energy that enables the *nephesh* to move.

When the *nephesh* achieves all it desires, it is filled or sated. It must be filled daily with meat and drink ("give us this day our daily bread"). If a man is hungry, his soul is empty. Meat and drink determine the growth of the *nephesh* to such an extent that desire of anything is called hunger and thirst (e. g. "my soul thirsts for the living God"). Although the Hebrews were able to distinguish between the *nephesh* and the body *(basar = flesh),* they were considered to be so intimately united that the body was thought of as the *nephesh* in its outward form.

All that supports the life of the *nephesh* was considered to be intimately related with the most important functions of the body. Hence breath *(ruach)* is intimately connected with life and *nephesh.* Yahweh breathed into the clay and made it a living *nephesh.* Blood for the Hebrew was also the source of life.[3] When a man dies his life drains away with the blood. The Hebrews are forbidden to eat meat which contains this sacred element in it.

The Hebrews thought of death as a weakening of the *nephesh.* The soul maintains its intimate relation to the body and so pervades the tomb in which the body is placed. Hence the mutilation of dead bodies and the destruction of tombs was (and is) a serious affront to the Hebrews. Even today the Arabs hold portions of Jerusalem; Jewish graveyards have been desecrated for this reason.

B. Corporateness.

To further understand the classical Hebrew concept of the status of the dead, it is necessary to understand the Hebrew concept of corporateness. Firstly, the relationship between Sheol and a grave cannot be explained with our present concept of space. Sheol was thought to be deep under the earth, graves were not, yet graves are in Sheol. Sheol is an entity into which all graves merged, and yet each grave maintains a measure of individuality.

Each grave is an expression of "Sheolness." For the Hebrew there was no such thing as an individual grave *per se,* nor was there such a thing as an individual tree. There were only single examples of "Sheolness" and "treehood." This is a fine distinction, but one that is important to understand. Where there is a grave, there all of Sheol is represented, where Sheol is, there are all graves.

The dead and decaying corpse was for the Hebrew an outward expression of a weakened *nephesh.* The *nephesh* is not bound or limited spacially merely to the confines of the corpse. Just as in life the *nephesh,* as representing the totality of a man, can go beyond the body into his possessions, so in death the *nephesh* may exist in part away from the corpse drifting about in the darkness of Sheol. Life does not suddenly cease at death; it continues in a weakened, decaying, darkened state. That which happens through normal death is, therefore, only that a kinsman passes from one department of the family to another. His soul lives among the shades of Sheol, but its substance (its power, its influence) is still acting in the blessing given by the elders of a family just before their death (cf. Isaac's blessing of Jacob and Esau). As long as the elder's memory lives, his personality is effective. However, it generally dwindles more and more until at last he is merged entirely in the great stock of life which upholds the family, that which is called the fathers. From them he has sprung and to them he returns.[4]

C. The Hebrew Concept of Flesh.

The Hebrews had no word for "body." Their closest equivalent is the word *basar.* It is best translated as "flesh." To the Hebrew *basar* stood for the whole life-substance as it was organized in corporeal form. Furthermore any part of the body could stand for the body as a whole. To say "My knees are weak" simply meant "I am afraid." The previously discussed idea of corporateness was also applied to the *basar.* This "flesh-body" was not what partitioned a man from his neighbor, it was rather something that bound him into the bundle of life with all men and nature.

D. Review of Historical Events in the 6th, 7th, and 8th centuries B. C.

1. The 8th century prophets (Amos, Hosea, Isaiah, & Micah) were writing in protest against the idea that Israel was due

special consideration from Yahweh because of the covenant relationship. They said that Yahweh's conscience transcended national boundaries. Because he has known her better than the surrounding nations he will punish her for her internal political corruption and social injustices. The prediction was made that God would use Assyria to punish Israel. The center of this prophecy was chiefly in Judah.

2. In 734 Pekah, King of Israel, and Rezin, King of Aram, attacked Ahaz, King of Judah, because his father Jotham refused to join their coalition against Assyria in 738. Ahaz appealed to Assyria for help, sending the entire wealth of the Temple and the royal palace. Ahaz became a vassal of Tiglath-Pilezer III. Damascus, the Capitol of Aram (Syria), was stormed by the Assyrians and fell in 732. In 733 Tiglath-Pilezer III conquered the Plain of Sharon, Galilee, and Gilead. He became King of Babylon under the name Pul.
3. In 721 Israel fell to Assyria and its inhabitants were deported. After the death of Jeraboam II Israel declined rapidly under a succession of 6 weak kings in 25 years.
4. 711 B. C. Revolt of Philistine city-states. Ashdod and the coastal plain fell to Assyria.
5. In 705 upon the death of Sargon II, King of Assyria, Hezekiah (King of Judah) rebelled against Assyria. The remnant of Samaria joined him.
6. In 701 Sennacherib, King of Assyria, campaigned against Judah. He shut up Hezekiah in Jerusalem "like a bird in a cage," but he failed to take the city either:
   a. Because a plague wiped out his army, or
   b. A sudden revolt in Babylonia required the withdrawal of his troops, or
   c. The Egyptian strength nearby prohibited him from making the attempt.
7. Isaiah was an unmoved center of calm in Jerusalem during these troubled times. Since his prediction that Jerusalem would not fall proved to be correct, his words along with those of Amos, Hosea and Micah were preserved.
8. This threat to Judah's security (the fall of nearby Israel and the hostility of Sennacherib) as well as the words of

the 8th century prophets, produced a sort of reform. This is known as Hezekiah's reform (cf. 2K 18:1-8). The reign of Hezekiah was prosperous and good.

9. Then followed the long reign of Manasseh (55 years, 697-642). At this time Assyria was at the peak of its power under Asshurbanipal. Manasseh's reign was one of concessions to the Assyrians and progressive loss of Judah's independence. Worship of Mesopotamian gods was introduced (The Queen of Heaven). This was a reactionary and a bad reign. Manasseh was the 'Judas of the Jews,' cf. 2K 21:16 "Moreover Manasseh shed very much innocent blood, till he had filled Jerusalem from one end to the other." The Asherah, the worship of the Assyrian pantheon of gods, and the offering of first-born sons, represent a return to the worst practices of Judah in the past. In the old days this conduct was naive and unthinking – but here it is consciously performed.
10. In that long reign there existed a few loyal people who had lived in the reign of Hezekiah and who listened to the prophets. They wrote down what the 8th century prophets had said and incorporated this into a law which became the book of Deuteronomy.
11. Manasseh's son Amon ruled for two years and then Josiah came to the throne in 640 at the age of 8. He ruled for about 31 years. Sometime during his reign (626-620?) the Scythians (a band of marauders from the Caucasian Mts.) came through Mesopotamia to Egypt. They did not harm the larger cities of Judah but they did frighten the Hebrews. The prophets and reformers got a better hearing. The time was right for reform. Also, Josiah was only a boy, his tutors were learned priests and were probably affected by prophetic teaching. A reform was inauguarated which was much more thorough than that of Hezekiah.
12. Jeremiah was born c. 645 in Anathoth, a small town, 4-5 miles northeast of Jerusalem. He was a man of property, of a relatively high social position, respected in the community, learned, unmarried. This combination was unusual for a Jew in the 7th century.
13. In the meanwhile significant changes were taking place in

the international situation. Asshurbanipal was Assyria's last great king. The power of Assyria declined seriously after his death in 625. Even before his death trouble had been brewing for Assyria with an attempted revolt by Babylon and growing Egyptian power. With great speed rumors of Assyrian weakness spread through the Fertile Crescent and caused restlessness among the satellite nations.

14. 626 ("In the 13th year of the reign of Josiah") Jeremiah began to preach. Chaldea, under Nabopolasser, declared its independence.
15. Things went from bad to worse and in 612 B. C. the Assyrian capital of Nineveh fell before the combined assault of the Babylonians, Medes, and Scythians. Nahum prophesied in this period.
16. Suddenly Egypt under Pharaoh Necho (609-593) decided to come to the rescue of Assyria. It was expedient to have a weak Assyria as a buffer against potential foes north of the Caucasus. Necho was also eager to bring Syria and Palestine back into Egypt's orbit of power.
17. In 609 B. C. Necho's army marched north to salvage the last remnants of the Assyrian Empire. He was intercepted at the pass of Magiddo by Josiah who gambled on achieving his goal of a united kingdom by throwing in his lot with the Babylonians (who would treat the Hebrews kindly during the Babylonian exile, showing that Josiah had gaged them correctly). Josiah was killed in the battle and Judah was without a competent leader.
18. 608 – Jeremiah preaches a sermon in the Temple which results in his banishment. The sermon is Chapter 7 of Jeremiah.
19. Necho continued his march to the Euphrates to challenge Babylonia. The issue was decided in 605 at the Battle of Carchemish when Necho and the Assyrians were defeated by the Medes and the Babylonians under Nebuchadnezzar.
20. 604 – Jeremiah wrote a book which King Jehoiakim of Judah burned. See Jer. 36.
21. 603 – Baruch wrote another book which underlies Jer. Chaps. 1-18.
22. 608 – 598 Rule of Jehoiakim who was appointed by

Pharaoh Necho. After Necho's defeat Jehoiakim switched allegiance to Nebuchadnezzar. Jehoiakim rebelled against Nebuchadnezzar in 598 but died before he could be chastized.

23. 597 – Jerusalem captured by the Babylonians and spared. Deportation of leading citizens (including Ezekiel) to Babylon.
24. 597 – 586 Judah under the rule of Zedekiah, a weak king.
25. 596 – Jerusalem captured by the Babylonians & demolished. 2nd deportation.
26. After 586 Gedaliah was governor of Palestine. He was murdered by Ishmael with the aid of the Ammonites and Egyptians.

[1]Cf. Gen. 12:5 "And Abram took Sarai his wife, and Lot his brother's son and all the substance that they had gathered *and the souls they had gotten in Haran;* and they went forth to go into the land of Canaan."

When a census was taken in Israel, the question asked was, "How many souls are there?"

Not only man, but animals in their total essence are souls. Cf. "And Yahweh said let the waters bring forth abundantly the moving *nephseh* that has life." (Gen. 1:20)

The Priestly source (P) states that Yahweh's covenant is not only between himself and the Hebrews, but between himself and their animals. E.g. "Behold I establish my covenant with you and your descendants after you, and with every living creature that is with you, the birds, the cattle, and every beast of the earth with you, as many as came out of the ark." (Gen. 9:10, 11).

[2]Ruach

[3]Cf. Cain and Abel – "The voice of your brother's blood is crying to me from the ground.

[4]The ideas expressed in sections A and B are taken from *Israel*, by Johs. Pederson, published by Oxford University Press, London and Branner Og Kerch, Copenhagen, 1926.

Chapter XVI

AMOS THE PROPHET.

A. The Rise of Prophecy.

The rise of classical prophecy began in Israel in the 8th century B. C. and it remained the center of Hebrew religious expression for about 200 years. It is important to understand that prophets were not men who had the ability to foretell the future. They were men in whom the Spirit of Yahweh was found and who thus were able to bring the message of God into history. A prophet was a man who could say with authority, "Thus says Yahweh." He often was able to make some cogent statement about the future of history – not because he had some special clairvoyance, but because of a common sense appraisal of the present situation was able to see its inevitable consequences. The first great prophet was Amos,[1] a native of Judah who prophesied against the northern Kingdom of Israel. He was the only prophet from the south who spoke out against the north. He was a shepherd and a vinedresser. His prophetic activity took place between 760 and 750 B. C. when Jeroboam II was ruling the northern kingdom.

Amos was a native of Tekoa which was little more than a spot on the map about 10 miles south of Jerusalem, but near the main trade route that ran from Egypt to Mesopotamia through the center of Israel and Judah. He must have learned of the decadent conditions in Israel from traders, and also from his own visits to Bethel, the southernmost sanctuary site in Israel.

One of the hallmarks of a prophet was the uniqueness of his call to prophecy. Samuel heard it in the voice of Yahweh which he mistook for the voice of Eli, Moses experienced it at the burning bush, Hosea felt it in the tragedy of his personal life. Isaiah was overpowered by a mystical experience in the Temple and Jeremiah's call was in the form of a conviction that this is what he was required to do in spite of his protest, "I am only a youth."

The call of Amos was quite dramatic. It can be reconstructed from his writing. One night when he was alone tending the sheep the silence was shattered by the roar of a lion as it seized its prey. Amos was too terrified to move, but in the morning he discovered at the scene of violence "two shinbones and the scrap of an ear."

He interpreted this event symbolically. The roar of the lion was the threat of Assyria and the defenseless sheep was Israel. Within this threatening voice he also felt the wrath of Yahweh compelling him to act. As a result he travelled northward through Israel reciting his forebodings of doom in the market places, in the holy places of worship, and in the social gatherings of the upper classes. He shocked his hearers – was resented, despised, hated, and ordered to leave.

B. Annotated Amos

The following is a presentation of the book of Amos listed in two columns with footnotes. The left column represents the original source, sayings of Amos which were probably memorized by him and eventually recorded. The right hand column contains material that was added later for several reasons. The footnotes are self explanatory.

Original Amos	Later Sources

YAHWEH'S WRATH IS UPON EVIL NATIONS

	1 The words of Amos, who was among the shepherds of Tekoa, which he saw concerning Israel in the days of Uzziah king of Judah and in the days of Jeroboam the son

Original Amos	Later Sources
	of Joash, king of Israel, two years before the earthquake.[a] 2 He said: When Yahweh thunders out of Zion, loudly from Jerusalem, then are the pasture-lands woe-begone, the ridge of Karmel withers.[b]
3 Thus says Yahweh: "After crime upon crime of Damascus I will not revoke the punishment; because they drove over the Gileadites, on threshing harrows with teeth of iron. 4 Therefore I will set fire to the house of Hazael, and it shall consume the palaces of Ben-Hadad; 5 I will even crash through the gates of Damascus, spreading confusion of battle through the city; I will exterminate the inhabitants from Biquath-Aven, and those who wield sceptres from Beth-Eden;	
	and the people of Syria shall go into exile to Kir.[c]
Yahweh has spoken.	
	6 Thus says Yahweh: "After crime upon crime of Gaza I will not revoke the punishment; because they carried into exile a whole people to deliver them up to Edom.

Original Amos	Later Sources

7 So I will send a fire upon
the wall of Gaza,
and it shall devour her strongholds.
8 I will cut off the inhabitants from Ashdod,
and him that holds the
scepter from Ashkelon;
I will turn my hand against
Ekron; and the remnant of
the Philistines shall perish,"
says Yahweh.

9 Thus says Yahweh:
"After crime upon crime
of Tyre I will not revoke
the punishment;
because they delivered up
a whole people to Edom,
and did not remember the
covenant of brotherhood.
10 So I will send a fire upon
the wall of Tyre,
and it shall devour her
strongholds."

11 Thus says Yahweh:
"After crime upon crime
of Edom I will not revoke
the punishment; because
he pursued his brother
with the sword,
and cast off all pity,
and his anger tore perpetually,
and he kept his wrath forever.

Original Amos	Later Sources
	12 So I will send a fire upon Teman, and it will devour the strongholds of Bozrah."[d]
13 Thus says Yahweh: "After crime upon crime of the Ammonites I will not revoke the punishment; because women with child they ripped up in Gilead, for the sake of enlarging their boundaries. 14 Therefore I will set fire to the walls of Rabbah, and it shall consume the palaces thereof;	
	with a war-cry in time of battle, with a blast in the day of the tempest; 15 and their king shall go into exile, he and his princes together."[e]
Yaweh has spoken.	

2

Thus says Yahweh:
"After crime upon crime of Moab I will not revoke the punishment;
because the bones of the

Original Amos	Later Sources
king of Edom, they have burned even into lime. 2 Therefore I will send into Moab a fire that shall consume the palaces of Kerioth;	
	then Moab shall die with an uproar, with an alarm at the trumpet's blast;
3 I will banish the judge from her midst, and slay all her princes with him." Yahweh has spoken.	
	4 Thus says Yahweh: "After crime upon crime of Judah I will not revoke the punishment; because they have rejected the law of Yahweh, and have not kept his statutes, led astray by their false gods, by idols that their ancestors had followed; 5 so I fling fires of war on Judah, to burn up the palaces of Jerusalem."[f]
6 Thus says Yahweh: "After crime upon crime of Israel I will not revoke the punishment; because they have sold the righteous for silver, and the needy for a pair of	

Original Amos

shoes.
7 They trample upon the heads of the poor,
the meek are denied access to the courts.
A father and his son go to the same woman,
and so my holy name is profaned;
8 sprawled out, they lie beside every altar,
even upon garments taken in pledge;
gulping down, in the house of their god,
the wine left as payment for penance."

Later Source

9 "Yet I destroyed the Amorite before them,
whose height was like the height of the cedars,
and who was as strong as the oaks;
I destroyed his fruit above,
and his roots beneath.
10 Also I brought you up out of the land of Egypt,
and led you forty years in the wilderness,
to possess the land of the Amorite.
11 And I raised up some of your sons for prophets,
and some of your young men for Nazirites.
Is it not indeed so, O people of Israel?"
says Yahweh.

Original Amos	Later Sources
	12 "But you made the Nazirites drink wine, and commanded the prophets, saying, 'You shall not prophesy.'[g]
	13 "Behold, I will press you down in your place, as a cart full of sheaves presses down.
	14 Flight shall perish from the swift, and the strong shall not retain his strength, nor shall the mighty save his life;
	15 he who handles the bow shall not stand, and he who is swift of foot shall not save himself, nor shall he who rides the horse save his life;
	16 and he who is stout of heart among the mighty shall flee away naked in that day," says Yahweh.[h]

EVERY EVENT IS PRECEDED BY A CAUSE

3 Hear this word which Yahweh has spoken against you, O people of Israel,	
	against the whole family which I brought up out of the land of Egypt:[i]
2 "You only have I known of all the families of the earth; therefore I will punish you	

Original Amos	Later Sources
for all your iniquities.	
3 "Do two walk together, unless they have made an appointment?	
4 Does a lion roar in the forest, when he has no prey? Does a young lion cry out from his den, if he has taken nothing?	
5 Does a bird fall in a snare on the earth, when there is no trap for it? Does a snare spring up from the ground, when it has taken nothing?	
6 Is a trumpet blown in a city, and the people are not afraid? Does evil befall a city, unless Yahweh has done it?	
	7 Surely the Lord Yahweh does nothing, without revealing his secret to his servants the prophets.[j]
8 The lion has roared; who will not fear? The Lord Yahweh has spoken; who can but Prophesy?"	

YAHWEH WILL SMITE ISRAEL.

Original Amos	Later Sources
9 Make proclamation upon the fortresses in Assyria, and upon the citadels in the land of Egypt, saying,	

Original Amos	Later Sources
"Assemble for battle against Mount Samaria, and behold the wild panic in her midst."	
	10 "They do not know how to do right," says Yahweh, "those who store up violence and robbery in their strongholds." 11 Therefore thus says the Lord Yahweh: "An adversary shall surround the land, and bring down your defenses from you, and your strongholds shall be plundered."[k]
12 Thus Yahweh has spoken: "As a shepherd snatches from the lion's mouth but two shin-bones or the scrap of an ear, so shall the people of Israel who dwell in Samaria be rescued, with nothing left but a bedpost, or a piece of silk from a divan."	
	13 "Hear, and testify against the house of Jacob." says the Lord Yahweh, the God of hosts, 14 "that on the day I punish Israel for his transgressions, I will punish the altars of

Original Amos | Later Sources

Bethel,
and the horns of the altar
shall be cut off
and fall to the ground.[1]

15 I will shatter the winter-house, as well as the summer cottage;
the palaces of ivory also shall be destroyed,
even the great mansions shall come to an end."
Yaweh has spoken.

4 Listen to these words -
You cows of Bashan,
Who are in Mount Samaria;
Who oppress the poor,
Who crush the needy,
Who say to your husbands,
"Serve and let us drink."

2 Yahweh has sworn by his holiness, that, "Behold, days shall come upon you

When you shall be dragged by the nose with hooks,
And by your buttocks, with fish spears;

3 Even as dung you shall be hauled out,
one by one,
To be cast forth on the dump heap naked."
A decree of Yahweh.
4 "Come to Bethel and transgress;
to Gilgal and multiply transgression;
bring your sacrifices every morning,

Original Amos

your tithes every three days;
5 offer a sacrifice of thanksgiving of that which is leavened,
and proclaim freewill offerings, publish them;
for so you love to do, O people of Israel!"
says the Lord Yahweh.

YAHWEH'S CHASTISEMENT HAS NOT BROUGHT REPENTANCE.

6 "I gave you cleanness of teeth in all your cities,
and lack of bread in all your places,
yet you did not return to me,"
says Yahweh.

7 "And I also withheld the rain from you when there were yet three months to the harvest;

Later Sources

I would send rain upon one city,
and hold it from another,
one patch would get rain,
and the rainless patch dried up,
8 till two or three towns would crawl to another in quest of water, all in vain;[m]

Original Amos

yet you did not return to me,"
says Yahweh.

Original Amos | Later Sources

9 "I smote you with blight and mildew;
I laid waste your gardens and your vineyards;

your fig trees and your olive trees
the locust devoured;[n]

yet you did not return to me."
says Yahweh.

10 "I sent among you a pestilence

after the manner of Egypt;
I slew your young men with the sword;
I carried away your horses;[o]

and I made the stench of your camp go up into your nostrils;
yet you did not return to me,"
says Yahweh.

11 I sent you a shattering earthquake,

like God's own shattering of Sodom and Gomorrah,

till you could only escape like charred sticks snatched from the fire;
yet you did not return to me,"
says Yahweh.

Original Amos	Later Sources
12 "Therefore thus I will do to you, O Israel;	
	because I will do this to you, prepare to meet your God, O Israel!"
	13 For lo, he who forms the mountains, and creates the wind, and declares to man what is his thought; who makes the morning darkness, and treads on the heights of the earth - Yahweh, the God of hosts, is his name![p]
5 Hear this word which I take up over you in lamentation, O house of Israel: 2 "Fallen, no more to rise, is the virgin Israel; forsaken on her land, with none to raise her up."	
	3 For thus says the Lord Yahweh; "The city that went forth a thousand shall have a hundred left, and that which went forth a hundred shall have ten left to the house of Israel."[q]

SEEK YAHWEH AND LIVE.

Original Amos	Later Sources
4 For thus says Yahweh to the house of Israel: "Seek me and live; 5 but do not seek Bethel, and do not enter into Gilgal or cross over to Beer-sheba;	
	for Gilgal shall surely go into exile, and Bethel shall come to nought."[r]
6 Seek Yahweh and live, lest he break out like fire in the house of Joseph, and it devour, with none to quench it for Bethel,	
	for Bethel,
7 O you who turn justice to wormwood, and cast down righteousness to the earth!	
	8 He who made the Pleiades and Orion, and turns deep darkness into the morning, and darkens the day into night, who calls for the waters of the sea, and pours them out upon the surface of the earth, Yahweh is his name, 9 who makes destruction flash forth against the strong, so that destruction comes upon the fortress.[s]

Original Amos	Later Sources

"YOU WILL NOT ENJOY YOUR PROSPERITY"

10 They hate him who reproves in the gate,
and they abhor him who speaks the truth.
11 Therefore because you trample upon the poor
and take from him exactions of wheat,
you have built houses of hewn stone,
but you shall not dwell in them;
you have planted pleasant vineyards,
but you shall not drink their wine.
12 For I know how many are your transgressions,
and how great are your sins - -
you who afflict the righteous, who take a bribe,
and turn aside the needy in the gate.

13 Therefore he who is prudent will keep silent in such a time;
for it is an evil time.

14 Seek good, and not evil, that you may live;
and so Yahweh, the God of hosts,
will be with you, as you have said.

15 Hate evil, and love good,

Original Amos	Later Sources
	and establish justice in the gate; it may be that Yahweh, the God of hosts, will be gracious to the remnant of Joseph.[t]
16 Therefore thus says Yahweh, the God of hosts, the Lord: "In all the squares there shall be wailing; and in all the streets they shall say, 'Alas! alas!'" They shall call the farmers to mourning and to wailing those who are skilled in lamentation,	
	17 and in all vineyards there shall be wailing, for I will pass through the midst of you," says Yahweh.[u]
18 Woe unto you who long for the day of Yahweh! What will this Day of Yahweh have in store for you? 19 It will be as when a man flees from the presence of a lion, and a bear meets him; then he comes home and leans his hand against the wall, and a serpent bites him.	

Original Amos	Later Sources
	20 Is not the day of Yahweh darkness, and not light, and gloom with no brightness in it?[v]

YAHWEH CANNOT BE 'BOUGHT OFF'

Original Amos	Later Sources
21 "I hate, I despise your feasts, and I take no delight in your solemn assemblies. 22 Even though you offer me your burnt offerings and cereal offerings, I will not accept them, and the peace offerings of your fatted beasts I will not look upon. 23 Take away from me the noise of your songs; to the melody of your harps I will not listen. 24 But let justice roll down like waters, and righteousness like an ever-flowing stream.	
	25 "Was it sacrifice and offering you brought me, all the forty years within the desert, Israel? 26 So now you must shoulder your king Sakkut, and Kaiwan your star-god, idols you have manufactured; 27 for into exile I send you,

Original Amos	Later Source
	far beyond Damascus," says Yahweh, whose name is the God of hosts.[w]

WOE TO THE SYBARITES

6 Woe to those who are at ease in Ephraim, and self-confident in Mount Samaria, the notable men of the first of the nations, to whom the house of Israel come!	
	2 Pass over to Calneh, and see; and thence go to Hamath the great; then go down to Gath of the Philistines. Are they better than these kingdoms? Or is their territory greater than your territory,[x]
3 Who give no thought to a day of reckoning, and spend their time practicing violence; 4 who recline upon beds made of ivory, and lie sprawled out on their couches; who eat the choice lambs from the flock, and calves from the midst of the stall; 5 Who thrum on the strings of the guitar, as they croon their dis-	

Original Amos	Later Sources
solute songs; 6 who gulp down their wine by the bowlful, and use the fine oil for cosmetics,	
	but are not grieved over the ruin of Joseph! 7 Therefore they shall now be the first of those to go into exile, and the revelry of those who stretch themselves shall pass away."[y]
8 The Lord Yahweh has sworn by himself	
	(says Yahweh, the God of hosts):[z]
"I abhor the pride of Jacob, and hate his strongholds; and will deliver up the city and all that is in it."	
	9 And if ten men remain in one house, they shall die. 10 And when a man's kinsman, he who burns him, shall take him up to bring the bones out of the house, and shall say to him who is in the innermost parts of the house, "Is there still anyone with you?" he shall say, "No"; and he shall say, "Hush! We must not mention the name of Yahweh."[aa]

Original Amos	Later Sources

11 For behold, Yahweh commands, and the great house shall be smitten into fragments,
and the little house into bits.
12 Do horses run upon rocks?
Does one plow the sea with oxen?
But you have turned justice into poison and the fruit of righteousness into wormwood –
you who rejoice over nothing,
who say, "Have we not by our own strength
taken Karnaim for ourselves?"
14 For behold, I will raise up against you a nation,
O house of Israel," says Yahweh, the God of hosts;
"and they shall oppress you from the entrance of Hamath
to the brook of the Arabah."

7 Thus the Lord Yahweh showed me: behold, he was forming locusts in the beginning of the shooting up of the latter growth; and lo, it was the latter growth after the king's mowings.

Original Amos	Later Sources
	2 When they had finished eating the grass of the land I said, "O Lord Yahweh, forgive, I beseech thee! How can Jacob stand? He is so small!" 3 Yahweh repented concerning this; "It shall not be," said Yahweh. 4 Thus the Lord Yahweh showed me: behold the Lord Yahweh was calling for a judgement by fire, and it devoured the great deep and was eating up the land. 5 Then I said, "O Lord Yahweh, cease, I beseech thee! How can Jacob stand? He is so small!" 6 Yahweh repented concerning this: "This also shall not be," said the Lord Yahweh 7 He showed me: behold, Yahweh was standing beside a wall built with a plumb line, with a plumb line in his hand. 8 And Yahweh said to me, "Amos, what do you see?" And I said, "A plumb line." Then Yahweh said, "Behold, I am setting a plumb

Original Amos	Later Sources
	line in the midst of my people Israel; I will never again pass by them;
9 the high places of Isaac shall be made desolate, and the sanctuaries of Israel shall be laid waste, and I will rise against the house of Jeroboam with the sword."	

AMOS IS RUN OUT OF TOWN.

10 Then Amaziah the priest of Bethel sent to Jeroboam king of Israel, saying, "Amos has conspired against you in the midst of the house of Israel; the land is not able to bear all his words.
11 For thus Amos has said, 'Jeroboam shall die by the sword, and Israel must go into exile away from his land.'"
12 And Amaziah said to Amos, "O seer, go, flee away to the land of Judah, and earn your living there; play the prophet there,
13 but never again prophesy at Bethel, for it is the king's sanctuary, and it is a temple of the kingdom."
14 Then Amos answered Amaziah, "I am no prophet, nor a prophet's son;

Original Amos | Later Sources

but I am a herdsman, and a dresser of sycamore trees, and Yahweh took
15 me from following the flock, and Yahweh said to me, 'Go prophesy to my people Israel.'
16 "Now therefore hear the word of Yahweh.
You say, 'Do not prophesy against Israel, and do not preach against the house of Isaac.'
17 Therefore thus saith Yahweh:
'Your wife shall be a harlot in the city,
and your sons and daughters shall fall by the sword,
and your land shall be parceled out by line;
you yourself shall die in an unclean land.

and Israel shall surely go into exile away from its land.' "[a b]

A LOOK AHEAD

8 Thus the Lord Yahweh showed me:
behold a basket of summer fruit.
2 And he said, "Amos, what do you see?" And I said, "A basket of summer fruit." Then Yahweh said to me,

Original Amos	Later Sources

"The end has come upon
my people Israel;
I will never again pass
by them.
3 The songs of the temple
shall become wailings in
that day,"
says the Lord Yahweh;
"the dead bodies shall be
many;
in every place they shall be
cast out in silence."
4 Hear this, you who trample
upon the needy,
and bring the poor of the
land to an end,
5 saying, "When will the
new moon be over,
that we may sell grain?
And the sabbath,
that we may offer wheat
for sale,
that we may make the
ephah small
and the shekel great,
and deal deceitfully with
false balances,
6 that we may buy the poor
for silver
and the needy for a pair of
sandals,
and sell the refuse of the
wheat?"
7 Yahweh has sworn by the
pride of Jacob:
"Surely I will never forget
any of their deeds.
8 Shall not the land tremble

on this account,
and every one mourn who dwells in it,
and all of it rise like the Nile,
and be tossed about and sink again, like the Nile of Egypt?"

9 "And on that day," says the Lord Yahweh,
"I will make the sun go down at noon,
and darken the earth in broad daylight.

10 I will turn your feasts into mourning,
and all your songs into lamentation;
I will bring sackcloth upon all loins,
and baldness on every head;
I will make it like the mourning for an only son,
and the end of it like a bitter day.

11 "Behold, the days are coming,"
says the Lord Yahweh,
"when I will send a famine on the land;
not a famine of bread, nor a thirst for water,
but of hearing the words of Yahweh.

Original Amos	Later Sources
	12 They shall wander from sea to sea, and from north to east; they shall run to and fro, to seek the word of Yahweh, but they shall not find it. 13 "In that day the fair virgins and the young men shall faint for thirst. 14 Those who swear by Ashimah of Samaria, and say, 'As thy god lives, O Dan,' and, 'As the way of Beer-sheba lives,' they shall fall, and never rise again."[ac] 9 I saw Yahweh standing beside the altar, and he said: "Smite the capitals until the thresholds shake, and shatter them on the heads of all the people;[ad]

NO PLACE TO HIDE

Original Amos	Later Sources
and what are left of them I will slay with the sword; not one of them shall flee away, not one of them shall escape. 2 "Though they dig into	

Original Amos	Later Sources
Sheol, from there shall my hand take them; though they climb up to heaven, from there I will bring them down. 3 Though they hide themselves on the top of Carmel, from there I will search out and take them; and though they hide from my sight at the bottom of the sea, there I will command the serpent, and it shall bite them.	
	4 And though they go into captivity before their enemies, there I will command the sword, and it shall slay them; and I will set my eyes upon them for evil and not for good."
	5 Yahweh, God of hosts, he who touches the earth and it melts, and all who dwell in it mourn, and all of it rises like the Nile, and sinks again, like the Nile of Egypt; 6 who builds his upper chambers in the heavens,

and founds his vault upon the earth;
who calls for the waters of the sea,
and pours them out upon the surface of the earth –
Yahweh is his name.[ae]

YAHWEH PLAYS NO FAVORITES

7 "Are you not like the Ethiopians to me,
O people of Israel?" says Yahweh.
"Did I not bring up Israel from the land of Egypt,
and the Philistines from Caphtor and the Syrians from Kir?
8 Behold the eyes of the Lord Yahweh are upon the sinful kingdom,
and I will destroy it from the surface of the ground;

except I will not utterly destroy the house of Jacob,"
says Yahweh.

9 "For lo, I will command,
and shake the house of Israel among all the nations
as one shakes with a sieve,
but no pebble shall fall upon the earth.

Original Amos	Later Sources
	10 All the sinners of my people shall die by the sword, who say, 'Evil shall not overtake or meet us.' 11 "In that day I will raise up the booth of David that is fallen and repair its breaches, and raise up its ruins, and rebuild it as in the days of old; 12 that they may possess the remnant of Edom and all thc nations who are called by my name," says Yahweh who does this. 13 "Behold the days are coming," says Yahweh, "when the plowman shall overtake the reaper and the treader of grapes him who sows the seed; the mountains shall drip sweet wine, and all the hills shall flow with it. 14 I will restore the fortunes of my people of Israel, and they shall rebuild the ruined cities and inhabit them; they shall plant vineyards and drink their wine, and they shall make gardens and eat their fruit.

Original Amos	Later Sources
	15 I will plant them upon their land, and they shall never again be plucked up out of the land which I have given them," says Yahweh your God.[af]

Key to Translation

M – Moffat, James. A New Translation of the Bible. Published by Harper & Brothers.

RSV – Revised Standard Version.

W – Wolfe, Rolland Emerson. *Meet Amos and Hosea.* Published by Harper & Beothers, 1945.

In Moffatt "Yahweh" substituted for "The Eternal" and "The Lord" throughout

In RSV "Yahweh" substituted for "The Lord" and "The Lord Yahweh" substituted for "The Lord God" throughout

1:1	RSV
1:2	M
1:3a	RSV
1:3b	M
1:3c	RSV
1:3d – 1:5b	W
1:5c	RSV
1:5d	W
1:6a	RSV
1:6b	M
1:6c – 1:8	RSV
1:9a	RSV
1:9b	M
1:9c – 1:10	RSV
1:11a	RSV
1:11b	M
1:11c – 1:12	RSV
1:13a	RSV
1:13b	M
1:13c – 1:14	W
1:15a	RSV
1:15b	W
2:1a	RSV
2:1b	M
2:1c	RSV
2:1d – 2:3	W
2:4a	RSV
2:4b	M
2:4c	RSV
2:4d – 2:5	M
2:6a	RSV
2:6b	M
2:6c	RSV
2:6d – 2:8	W
2:9 – 2:16	RSV
3:1a	W
3:1b – 3:8	RSV
3:9	W
3:10 – 3:11	RSV
3:12	W
3:13 – 14	RSV
3:15	W
4:1 – 4:3	W
4:4 – 4:7a	RSV
4:7b – 4:8a	M
4:8b – 4:10	RSV
4:11a	M
4:11b – 4:13	RSV
5:1 – 5:17	RSV
5:18 – 5:19	W
5:20 – 5:24	RSV
5:25 – 5:27a	M
5:27b	RSV
6:1a	W
6:1b – 6:2	RSV
6:3 – 6:6a	W
6:6b – 6:14	RSV
7:1 – 7:12a	RSV
7:12b	M
7:13 – 7:17	RSV
8:1 – 8:14	RSV
9:1 – 9:15	RSV

[1]The Hebrews categorized the prophets canonically into two groups; The Former Prophets: Joshua, Judges, Samuel, and Kings, The Latter Prophet: Isaiah, Jeremiah, Ezekiel, and the 12 minor prophets. Amos was one of the minor prophets.

a[1] is a superscription added by editors to introduce the book (The violence of the earthquake can be seen in Zech. 14:5. It caused landslides that filled valleys.)

[b]1:2 is a part of the superscription. V.2a is similar to Joel 3:16a. It may have been copied from Joel which was probably written later than Amos.

[c]The exile to Kir occurred after the fall of Damascus and is described in 2K16:9. Damascus fell in 732 B. C., therefore 1:5c was added by later editors.

[d]The condemnation of the Philistine cities of Gaza, Ashdod, Ashkelon, and Ekron, the Phoenician city of Tyre and the land of Edom is not written in the forceful style of Amos. The fact that the Philistine city of Gath which fell in 711 B. C. is omitted from the list looks as though the author was writing after this event.

[e]The exile of the king of Ammon from the capital city of Rabbah is mentioned in Jeremiah 49:3 and may refer to the aftermath of the attack on the Ammonites by Nebuchadnezzar about 150 years after Amos.

[f]These two verses are a weak imitation of Amos' style. They were probably added by a post-Deuteronomic editor who was applying the prophecy to the fall of Judah. The denunciation is general and vague. Amos had a clear call to cry out against Israel. Judah was not involved in his message.

The 'law' and the 'statutes' are Deuteronomic concepts. The problem of idol worship was a serious one in post-Deuteronomic times.

[g]Vv. 9-12 concerning the destruction of the Amorites during the occupation of Palestine by the Israelites, the reference to the Exodus, and mention of the ancient sect of Nazirites represents an insertion of patriarchal history by a later editor. It has no direct bearing on the message of Amos.

[h]Vv. 13-16 are a later addition of apocalyptic material. The writer is looking forward to the day of God's rule. The words 'in that day' in v. 16 are a hallmark of apocalyptic writing.

[i]3:1b is clearly seen to be a gloss from the 'I' which occurs before the quotation of Yahweh begins.

[j]A gloss added as an elaboration on the preceding material.

[k]3:10, 11 is a gloss which attempts to develop Amos' theme that Yahweh will punish the wickedness of Israel. It is insipid compared to the material that brackets it.

[l]A weak gloss with a purpose similar to vv. 10 and 11.

[m]Vv. 7b-8a is a rambling gloss which attempts to highlight v. 7 but actually detracts from the original text.

[n]An editorial annotation that takes direct action away from Yahweh.

[o]An addition by a scribe interested in early history.

[p]The main purpose of v. 13 is to assert the monotheistic beliefs of post-exilic Israel and to emphasize the fact that it was Yahweh who created the universe. It was probably added by an editor to make up for the material in v. 12 that was excised. Its mildness is completely out of context with the fierce words of Amos.

[q]An inferior verse containing a trace of apocalypticism.

[r]The positiveness of 5:5b suggests that Gilgal may have already gone into exile.

[s]Vv. 8 and 9 were added by a later editor to counteract Amos' undeveloped monotheism which was embarrassing to the priestly writers. Amos' God of Justice is linked with the Creator of the Universe.

[t]Vv. 13-15 is a ruminating addition confirming and amplifying what Amos has said.

[u]An anticlimax when compared with v. 16

[v]An elaboration of v. 18

[w]Vv. 25-27 are a post-exilic addition to emphasize the opposition of a monotheistic religion to idol worship.

[x]If the reference here is to the defeat of Calneh, Hamath, and Gath by the Assyrians, v. 2 is a late addition since they were conquered between 738 and 711 B. C.

[y]The writing in vv. 6b and 7 is not as vivid as the descriptions immediately preceding and may be spurious.

[z]A gloss, redundant with v. 8a.

[aa]The meaning of vv. 9 and 10 is obscure. Perhaps it refers to burning the bodies during a plague. The vagueness of it disqualifies it as genuine Amos.

[ab]The three visions in 7:1-8 smack of apocalypticism. This places them after the time of Amos. The first two visions have an additional post-exilic element in that the crushing burden of Amos' prophesy is alleviated by the postulation of a repentant God. The third vision (that of the plumb line) contains a pun on the Hebrew words for 'plumb line' and 'grief.' The first two visions are clearly not original Amos, the pun make the third doubtful.

v. 17b is a gloss tacked on the end of the scathing reply of Amos to Amaziah when Amaziah orders him out of the country.

[ac]In general, the literary quality of chapter 8 is inferior to the original Amos. Several elements within it are clearly post-exilic. The vision of the basket of summer fruit contains a pun in addition to having an apocalyptic tinge – each of which makes the passage doubtful. V.3 contains the words 'in that day' which brands it as an apocalyptic writing. Vv. 4-6 are a poor echo of the original Amos in 2:6. In vv. 7 and 8 an earthquake is ineptly compared with the rise and fall of the Nile. V.9 is an apocalypse since it is introduced by 'and on that day.' The description of the darkness at noon is typical apocalyptic material. Vv. 10-14 are placed in the same category due to their emphasis on future events.

[ad]9:la describes a vision with an apocalyptic tinge and makes this half of the verse uncertain.

[ae]Vv. 4,5 and 6 are a mixture of the assertion of Yahweh the Creator and the forward look of the apocalyptic writer.

[af]Vv. 8b-10 represent an attempt to soften the harsh judgment of Amos by promising that some of Israel shall be saved. They are a message to a later day.

Vv. 11 and 12 refer to the Temple which fell in 586 B. C. They were added long after the time of Amos.

Vv. 13ff. refer to the return from the exile.

Chapter XVII

AMOS (continued) AND HOSEA

A. Amos' Teaching

The Hebrews in Amos' times needed to be freed from an increasing nationalism, i.e., the conviction that they were Yahweh's chosen people and no other nation was a part of God's plan in history. They also needed to be cleansed from the corruption that arose from the amalgamation of Yahweh and the baals. Amos believed that the Hebrews were mistaken in their idea that God could be bought off by sacrifices and that prosperity meant God's favor. The central theme of Amos is *righteousness*. The key verse is 5:24,

> "But let justice roll down like waters, and righteousness like an everflowing stream."

Amos' teaching can be summarized under two headings:

1. Yahweh's attitude towards other nations.

In denouncing foreign nations (cf. Amos 1:3ff.; 2:1ff.) Amos attracted attention to his preaching. But these condemnations were more than a device to startle his hearers. The important point is the reason given for Yahweh's punishment of these enemies in

Judaism. The reason is that God's conscience transcends national boundaries. The rabid nationalism of the Hebrews caused them to see Yahweh as the war god of Israel fighting against the gods of other nations. Amos saw Yahweh as a moral God offended at the immoral acts of any nation. What is right is right no matter where it is done. This was an important step in the development of Israel's religion.

This national god of Israel eventually came to be recognized by the Hebrews as a god of all nations. Amos shifted the ground from politics to morals. Since Yahweh was a moral god, the other deities eventually became superfluous. Amos' teaching becomes, therefore, a first step towards monotheism.

2. Yahweh's attitude towards Israel.

In these writings of Amos the conscience of Yahweh is operating, against his own people. If right is right, God demands it *especially* of his own people. Those who know what is right and persist in doing what is wrong are especially guilty. Amos speaks of Israel's sins of bribery, oppression of the poor, dishonesty in business, pride, indifference, and selfish luxury in the midst of want.

The pre-prophetic religion of the Hebrews needed to be freed from the belief that Yahweh's favor could be bought with sacrifices. Amos put the emphasis in religion where it belongs – not on pleasure but on common welfare. He saw that in Yahweh's eyes there is no substitute for a reformation in the character of the worshipper.

The pre-prophetic religion of the Hebrews also needed to be freed from the conviction that obedience to Yahweh leads to prosperity. When God operates, it is not always in terms of prosperity. Yahweh's conscience means trouble – "Woe to you who desire the day of the Lord!"

B. Additions to Amos.

It is not likely that Amos, a shepherd and vinedresser, wrote the original part of the book. Probably someone close to the events was interested enough to write them down. This material was then taken from Israel to Jerusalem, where it was preserved and studied by Isaiah. It was written c. 750 B. C. and became part of the canon c. 200 B. C. Many changes were made in these intervening years. Each new copyist adapted the material to the needs of his own day. The types of addition may be categorized as follows:

1. Changes from denunciation to hope. Amos was caustic and predicted that the Israelites' conduct would bring them to ruin. Hence 9:8a; 7:9; and 6:14 are genuine. However, about 400 B. C., after the Babylonian Exile, the Israelites needed a more hopeful word. Hence material such as 9:6b; 9:11; and 9:13ff. were added.
2. 5:8,9 and 9:5,6 were added to make Amos' theology monotheistic. The fact that it wasn't is seen in 9:3.
3. A denunciation of Judah was added. Amos' oracles were specific, but additions such as found in 2:4,5 are vague and general. "Law" and "statutes" are Deuteronomic concepts that came long after Amos.
4. Apocalyptic material was added. (cf. 2:13 ff.).
5. There were moralistic additions. (cf. 5:13-15).
6. Certain scribes who were interested in patriarchal history added verses such as 2:10 and 5:25.
7. Someone interested in visions added most of the material found in chapters 7,8, and 9.

C. Hosea

Hosea was a native of the northern kingdom (Israel), and the only important literary prophet that the ten northern tribes ever produced. His years of prophecy were c. 745-735 B. C. This places him at the end of the reign of the last great northern king, Jeroboam II, and at the beginning of the weak and rapid decline of his six successors.[1] Hosea was the only prophetic book written in Israel against the northern kingdom.

The text is the most corrupt of all the books of the Bible. This means that it had undergone the most number of changes: deletions, additions, and rearrangement of order.

The author was a prosperous farmer. The major tragedy of his life was the unfaithfulness of his wife Gomer. The genius of the book lies in his comparison of Gomer to the unfaithfulness of Yahweh. The theme of the book is that just as Yahweh bestows faithfulness and affection – so does he demand it. The key word in Hosea is *hesed* which is translated as *steadfast love.* The key verse is 6:6.

> "For I desire steadfast love and not sacrifice,
> the knowledge of God, rather than burnt offerings."

Hosea feels that the baals are intolerable. The worship of them instead of Yahweh is a denial of *hesed* on the part of the people.

As was Amos, so was Hosea opposed to political corruption. He also denounced alliances between the Hebrews and foreign nations. The Hebrews' sole alliance should be with Yahweh.

D. Additions to the Text

As is the case with Amos, many additions have been made to the original text of Hosea. Some of these arose as a result of an attempt to make the book applicable to Judah even though it was written to apply to Israel.[2] Some additions were an attempt to remove the curse of Hosea, which was too hard to bear.[3]

The additions of an idol-editor is also apparent.[4] All of chapter 12 is the work of someone interested in patriarchal history – "A pompous but muddled scribe."

E. Original Hosea

Original Hosea is as follows:

1:1ac, 2 (the Lord said to Hosea, "Go, take to yourself a wife . . . for the land commits great harlotry by forsaking the Lord), 3 – 6 (to "Not pitied"), 8,9.

2:2, 3, 5 – 13. (except 8c)

3:1 – 3.

4:1, 2, 4, 6a, 7, 9, 10a, 12a, 13, 14b, 15, 17, 18.

5:1 – 3a, 4b, 5ab, 6, 7a, 8, 9, 11 – 14 (Change "Judah" to "Israel").

6:4ac, 5bc, 6 – 10.

7:1b, 2, 3, 5 – 9, 11, 12, 13 (omit "I would redeem them, but"), 14, 15b, 16.

8: 2 – 4, 7 – 9, 10b – 13a, 14ac.

9: 1 – 4, 5 – 10a, 11, 12a, 13, 15, 16.

10:1 – 3, 7, 9 – 11, 13, 14a, 15.

11:1, 3 – 7.

13:3, 7 – 16.

In conclusion we may say that Hosea made a contribution to literary style in his time. He made more use of simile and metaphor than any other Old Testament author. He was the first to see Yahweh's qualities of long-suffering and steadfast love. He saved Judaism from the degeneracy of baal-worship.

[1]

Jeroboam II	786-746
Zechariah	746-745
Shallum	745
Menahem	745-738
Pekahiah	738-737
Pekah	737-732
Hoshea	732-721
Fall of Israel	721

[2] Cf. 1:7, 11; 4:15; 5:12-14 (all "Judahs" should read "Israel"; 6:11.

[3] Cf. 1:10, 11; 2:15, 16, 21-23; 3:4, 5; 5:15-6:3; 11:8-11.

[4] Cf. 2:8c; 8:4b-6; 9:10b; 10:5, 6, 8; 11:2b; 13:1, 2.

Chapter XVIII

FIRST ISAIAH. (CHAPTERS 1 – 39)

A. Prophecy in the Hebrew Canon.

Isaiah was the first of four prophetic books in the Hebrew Bible. These books were Isaiah, Jeremiah, Ezekiel, and the Twelve (i.e., minor prophets). These books were assembled long after prophecy had ceased. Originally the prophets made speeches (e. g., Elijah). After the time of Elijah, i. e., in the time of Amos, c. 750 B. C., the prophets' speeches began to be recorded, but probably not by themselves. They spoke in poetic verse and a disciple recorded his master's work (cf. Isaiah 8:16, Jeremiah 36:4). Later, about the time of Second Isaiah (Isaiah 40 – 66), c. 400 B. C., written prophecy took the place of spoken prophecy.

The words of the great prophets (Amos, Isaiah, Jeremiah, and Ezekiel) were accepted by the Hebrews as having been inspired by God. Hence later generations edited and amended the earlier prophetic writings to suit their current needs. Many passages were added promising hope for the future of Israel. These additions made it desirable to recover and reconstitute the orginal record of the sayings as was done with Amos in Chapter XVI. Original Isaiah is as follows:

1	9:8 - 10:4a	20:1 - 6
2:6 - 4:1	10:5 - 15a	22:1 - 14, 15 - 25
5	10:28 - 32	28:7 - 22
6	14:24 - 32	29:1 - 4, 9, 10, 13 - 15
7:1 - 16	17:1 - 3a	30:1 - 5, 8 - 19
8:1 - 18	18:1 - 6	31:1 - 3

B. Isaiah the Man.

Isaiah was a native of Judah (perhaps of Jerusalem). His ministry began "in the year that King Uzziah died." That was in 740 B. C. We do not know the date of Isaiah's death. His writings describe the course of events to 701 B. C., when Sennacherib, King of Assyria, campaigned against Judah and beseiged Jerusalem.

One of the hallmarks of a prophet was his "call." Each call was unique but contained common elements, viz., a vision of God's glory, a feeling of unworthiness, a sense of forgiveness, the realization of God's call and a response to it. Isaiah's call occurred while he was worshipping in the Temple in Jerusalem. It is described in Isaiah 6:1-8. King Uzziah had just died leaving his weak son Jotham, now the king, threatened by an Assyrian invasion. In such an hour Isaiah says "I saw *the* king," implying that the Hebrews ought not to be dependent upon the Davidic king enthroned in Jerusalem, but upon the true and only king, Yahweh, the Lord of Hosts. Isaiah was probably standing just inside the main door of the Temple where "the foundations of the thresholds shook at the voice of him who called." The seraphim refer to the two angels whose statues were on the Ark of the Covenant overshadowing the "mercy seat" or throne of Yahweh. The three pairs of wings symbolically express appropriate responses to Yahweh's presence. With one pair they shield their faces from the King's blinding glory. With the second pair they hide their nakedness[1] from his purity. With the third pair they fly to their appointed tasks.

The uncleanness of which Isaiah feels himself guilty, and of which he accuses the nation, is an uncleanness of the lips, that is to say, of speech, and consequently of the thoughts and feelings which speech can express. This is an indication of the important place which morality is to occupy in his thoughts. The touching of his lips with the live coal is symbolic of cleansing and dedication. Animal sacrifices were burned on the altar. The dedication of objects that would not burn was performed by touching the objects with a coal from the altar fire.

Isaiah felt himself called to proclaim the imminent ruin of all of Yahweh's people, including Judah, just as Amos and Hosea about this time were foretelling more especially of the overthrow of Israel. Apparently he thought that a remnant would be saved. Hence he named his son Shearjashub "a remnant shall return (to God)."

C. Isaiah and King Ahaz (cf. 2 Kings 16 and Isaiah 7).

In 734 B. C. Pekah, the king of Israel, and Rezin, king of Syria, attacked Ahaz, king of Judah, because his father Jotham did not join them in a revolt against Assyria in 737 B. C. Ahaz was prepared to appeal for help from Assyria. In his panic he sacrificed his son as an offering (2 Kings 16:3).

Isaiah confronted Ahaz as he was inspecting the water supply of Jerusalem at the end of the conduit leading to the upper pool. This was in preparation for the expected siege. Isaiah advised Ahaz to stand fast and rely on Yahweh.

> "Take heed, be quiet, do not fear, and do not let your heart be faint because of these two smoldering stumps of firebrands, at the fierce anger of Rezin and Syria and the son of Remaliah. Because Syria, with Ephraim and the son of Remaliah, has devised evil against you, saying, "Let us go up against Judah and terrify it, and let us conquer it for ourselves, and set up the son of Tabeel as king in the midst of it," thus says the Lord God:
>
> It shall not stand,
> and it shall not come to pass.
> For the head of Syria is Damascus,and the head of Damascus is Rezin.
>
> (Within sixty-five years Ephraim will be broken to pieces so that it will no longer be a people.)
>
> And the head of Ephraim is Samaria,
> and the head of Samaria is the
> son of Remaliah.
> If you will not believe,

surely you shall not be established.

Isaiah 7:4 - 9

Ahaz refused to ask a sign from Yahweh as Isaiah prompted him to do, ostensibly because he did not want to put the Lord to the test. Actually he probably did not want to hear what Yahweh would say lest it be against what he already had decided to do. In anger Isaiah replied,

> Therefore the Lord himself will give you a sign. Behold, a young woman shall conceive and bear a son, and shall call his name Immanuel.[2] He shall eat curds and honey when he knows to refuse the evil and choose the good. For before the child knows how to refuse the evil and choose the good, the land before whose two kings you are in dread will be deserted.
>
> Isaiah 7:14 - 16

The words "Behold a young woman shall conceive" – which was translated "behold a virgin shall conceive" in the King James Bible – have traditionally been taken to support the doctrine of the Virgin Birth and to apply to the expected Messiah. In the context in which they stand they have neither of these meanings. Adolphe Lods in his book *The Prophets and the Rise of Judaism* gives a clear account of the meaning of this passage:

> Before the birth of a child, conceived at the moment at which the prophet is speaking, that is to say within nine months, Judah will be delivered from the dreaded aggressors; and the child when it is born may be given the joyful name Immanuel, "God with us." But before this same child has learnt to refuse the evil and choose the good, that is to say to make use of its reasoning powers, in two or three years in fact, the kingdom of Judah, invaded by these same Assyrians whom in his folly the king summons to his help, and by

> their enemies the Egyptians, shall become a wilderness covered with brambles and thorns, whose few inhabitants, obliged to revert to their pastoral life, shall live on curds and wild honey."[3]

D. Isaiah and King Hezekiah.

Hezekiah, the son of Ahaz, became king of Judah in 715 B. C. He did not follow the policy of his father which was to appease Assyria and rule as a vassal of the Assyrian king. A series of reforms were instituted in Judah. Worship of foreign gods was outlawed, statues and altars to the baals were destroyed, and a strict observance of the Covenant was re-instituted. The city of Jerusalem was made less vulnerable to attack by the construction of the Siloam Tunnel, an underground aqueduct about 1780 feet long, leading from a spring outside of the city walls to the Pool of Siloam inside the walls.

In 711 B. C. a spirit of rebellion against Assyria arose in Philistia. It was encouraged by Egypt, who was opposed to Assyrian power. Isaiah was opposed to foreign intrigue and protested against it by walking for three years naked and barefoot through the streets of Jerusalem as a sign that Assyria would lead Egypt and Ethiopia naked into exile.[4] The Egyptians abandoned the Philistines before the revolt was concluded. Sargon, king of Assyria, destroyed Ashdod and converted Philistia into an Assyrian province. Hezekiah was not involved at that time, perhaps because he took Isaiah's advice to stay away from foreign alliances.

When Sargon died in 705 B. C. there was a chain reaction of revolutions throughout the Assyrian Empire. It began in Babylonia under King Marduk-apal-iddina (Biblical Merodach-baladan), spread across the Fertile Crescent, through Palestine where it coincided with a nationalistic revival of Egyptian power under Pharaoh Shabeko. Hezekiah joined the general uprising in spite of Isaiah's warning against it in the words:

> "In returning and rest you shall be saved; in quietness and in trust shall be your strength."
>
> Isaiah 30:15

Sennacherib, king of Assyria, defeated Marduk-apal-iddina, and then sought vengeance in Philistia. He destroyed a large Egyptian army at Ekrom, captured the Judean city of Lachish and beseiged Jerusalem. King Hezekiah sought Isaiah's advice. It was given in these words:

> Do not be afraid because of the words that you have heard (from the Rabshakeh, or chief steward of Sennacherib's army), with which the servants of the king of Assyria have reviled me. Behold I will put a spirit in him, so that he shall hear a rumor, and return to his own land; and I will make him fall by the sword in his own land."
>
> Isaiah 37:5 – 7

These are the last words we have from Isaiah. In 701 B. C. the Assyrian army mysteriously and suddenly ended the seige of Jerusalem.

E. A Step towards Monotheism.

Isaiah's ideas of the nature of God affirm those of Amos, who believed that Yahweh's justice extended beyond the borders of Israel. In writing "Assyria, the rod of my anger, the staff of my fury!" Isaiah saw that Assyria, although it thought of itself as an important and powerful nation, was simply an instrument in the hands of a righteous God. This was not a case of military might triumphing but a case of Yahweh using Assyria for his purposes, which are just – namely the punishment of a nation which had forsaken the Covenant.[5] This is a step towards monotheism.

F. Summary of Historical Application of the Prophecies of Isaiah.

1. Pekah, king of Israel, and Rezin, king of Damascus, declare war on Israel under king Ahaz (734 B. C.). Ahaz is about to appeal to Tiglath-Pileser III, king of Assyria. Read 2 Kings 16 and Isaiah 7.
2. Ahaz becomes a vassal of Tiglath-Pileser III from 734 B. C. Isaiah devotes his efforts towards restraining Israel and Judah from revolting against Assyria. They are not to rely upon their own strength, or that of alliances, but on Yahweh. At the time of the revolt of Hoshea, the last king of Israel, he writes Isaiah 18:1-6. This, referring to

Egypt, might apply to Shabako's invitation for Palestine to revolt.

3. 715 B. C. Philistia does not rejoice at the death of Ahaz, for if Judah doesn't oppress her, Assyria will. Cf. Isaiah 14:28-31.
4. Isaiah sets Hezekiah on his guard against Merodachbaladan of Babylon. Cf. 2 Kings 20:12-19 and Isaiah 39.
5. Isaiah warns against the intrigues of Shabako (711 B. C.). Cf. Isaiah 20; Isaiah 18:1-6.
6. Hezekiah is told not to appeal to Egypt for help against Assyria. Cf. Isaiah 30:1 – 7a; 31:1 – 5; 38:7-22.
7. The treasurer, Shebna, one of the leaders of the pro-Egyptian party, builds a sepulchre for himself near Jerusalem. Isaiah tells him he will die in a foreign land. Cf. Isaiah 22:15-18.
8. Isaiah supports Hezekiah's resistance during the seige of Jerusalem by Sennacherib. Cf. 2 Kings 19:20-34. Isaiah 31:8, 9; 37:5-7.
9. After the retreat of Sennacherib everyone is happy except Isaiah. The citizens of Jerusalem are hopelessly corrupt. Cf. Isaiah 22:1-14; 1:1-17.

[1] "Feet" may be a euphemism for the genitals.

[2] That is *God is with us.*

[3] *The Prophets and the Rise of Judiasm,* Adolphe Lods, Routledge and Kegan Paul Ltd., London and Dutton, New York, 1937, page 103.

[4] Cf. Isaiah 20.

[5] Cf. Isaiah 9:11-12a

So the Lord raises adversaries against them,
and stirs up their enemies.
The Syrians on the east and the Philistines on the west
devour Israel with open mouth.

Chapter XIX

DEUTERONOMY

A. Background to Deuteronomy

Deuteronomy represents a pivotal point in the Old Testament. In 701 B. C. Sennacherib had campaigned against Judah, shutting up King Hezekiah in Jerusalem "like a bird in a cage." Isaiah was the unmoved center of this whirlpool. His advice proved to be sound, and his words, with those of Amos, Hosea, and Micah, were preserved. In the time of Isaiah there was a threat to Judah's security which produced a sort of reform (cf. 2 Kings 18:1 – 8). The reign of Hezekiah was a good reign involving this reform.

Then came the long reign of Manasseh – a rule of 55 years (693 through 639 B. C.). Assyria was at the peak of its power under Asshurbanipal. Manasseh's reign was one of concessions to the Assyrians and a loss of Judah's independence. The Hebrews worshipped the gods of Mesopotamia (cf. 2 Kings 21:16).

In that long reign there remained a few faithful men who listened to the prophets. When Jerusalem was being saturated with innocent blood these men were in hiding. They recorded what the prophets had said and composed a law which included the ideas of the prophets. A few years later, after Manasseh died, they had their chance to be heard (Cf. 2 kings 21:19ff.).

The next king, Amon, ruled for two years and was murdered. Josiah ruled next, coming to the throne at the age of 8 years. He reigned from 640 to 609 B. C. In this period (during the early 620's), the Scythians, a band of marauders, came out of Mesopotamia towards Egypt. They didn't harm Judah, but they did frighten the Judeans. The prophets and reformers had a better hearing, just as they do during any crisis. The time was finally right for those who had been nurturing the prophetic position. Josiah's tutors were learned priests and were probably affected by the prophetic teaching, which, as we shall see, compose a large part of the Book of Deuteronomy.

B. Background to 2 Kings 22ff.

1. This account is by an eyewitness author of the finding of a book in the Temple which was short enough to be read twice in one day, and incited the king to reform (Cf. 2 Kings 22:8ff). The reforms are listed in Chapter 23; the Temple was cleansed, the Asherah cut down, the local sanctuaries were abolished and the pagan shrines demolished.

The Hebrews were admonished to keep the Passover, since this feast had been neglected since the time of the Judges. Mediums and wizards were cast out and the observance of the Law was re-established. Actually it is likely that the local sanctuaries in Judah had been falling to ruin for about a century, i. e., during the Assyrian campaign and following the reign of Hezekiah. Nevertheless Josiah gave the coup de grace.

2. 2 Kings 23:9 ("However, the priests of the high places did not come up to the altar of the Lord in Jerusalem, but they ate unleavened bread among their brethren") gives an important clue concerning the religious situation. The local priests had an opportunity to come to Jerusalem to minister, but they did not take it. What was "the book of law" which is mentioned in 2 Kings 22 and 23? Clearly it is the core of the Book of Deuteronomy.[1] The point by point prescriptions of Deuteronomy can be matched with 2 Kings 22ff.

C. Deuteronomy.

Deuteronomy was published in 621 B. C. (the 18th year of King Josiah). It can be divided into three parts, plus a supplement, as follows:

1.	1:1 - 4:43	An introduction which was added later.
2.	4:44 - 11	An introduction to the core.
	12 - 26	The Core.
	28	Conclusion to the core.
3.	29 - 30	A conclusion added later.
4.	27, 31 - 34	A supplement.

The bulk of chapters 12 through 26 seems to have been written shortly before the book was found. 2 Kings 22 tells how the book was put into circulation. This does not say that the book was found in the money box in the Temple, but this is a clear implication in 2 Chronicles 34:14.

D. A Pious Fraud?

Deuteronomy has been called "a pious fraud" because it consists of a series of speeches attributed to Moses and gives a program for a new land. It is far more likely, in fact it is almost certain, that the book was written by someone or some school of writers shortly before 621 B. C. who were interested in legal reform. It was ascribed to Moses because Moses was the great law-giver and also because some of the Deuteronomic Laws are clearly ancient.

The Hebrews were intellectually honest about this. It was not a case of plagiarism. There was no sense of historical discrimination. This was merely an enterprising way by which an unknown author secured a hearing.

E. Why is Deuteronomy Important?

1. Deuteronomy is the first embodiment of prophecy in a workable law. Its content does not represent the most advanced thought of the nation, but it does present a platform of morality for the average citizen. There is no feeling of rivalry between prophet and priest, but rather the idea that the priest is making the prophetic teachings an integral part of daily life. This in turn makes Deuteronomy the crown of the prophets' work.

2. Deuteronomy is important because of its effect on the life of the Hebrews. The prophets almost failed, but the ethical and moral guides of Deuteronomy governed the life of the nation for two centuries until the priestly codes (c. 450 B. C.) became the guide of life. The Deuteronomic Laws were not wholly en-

forced – no law code is – but at least they were recognized as a standard towards which every Hebrew felt an obligation to strive.

3. This is the place where the religion of Israel became the religion of a book. Previously the social situation was guided and governed by songs and oral phrases ("Saul has slain his thousands, and David his tens of thousands"), by oral tradition, by the spoken word of Moses, Joshua, and the judges. But now the civil law was written in a book. The beginning of a canon of Scripture began to emerge. Deuteronomy is a kind of specific cornerstone placed where the oral tradition had been.

4. Deuteronomy is the book which says that religion should be centralized in Jerusalem (cf. Deuteronomy 12:5). This was an important step towards the abolition of worship at the "high places." As a result no temples were built by the Hebrews during their exile in Babylon. The emphasis on Temple worship in Jerusalem gave the Temple priests prestige and power. Not only was the establishment of other priesthoods discouraged, but the religious leaders in Jerusalem had a considerable amount of control over the Hebrews when their kings were subservient to foreign powers. This position of importance remained in force even after the Babylonian exile.

Many of the "country priests" who were invited to come to Jerusalem did not take advantage of this offer. A century later when they tried to move their centers of worship there, they were denied.

5. Deuteronomy is essentially a combination of the teachings of prophets and priests. The danger inherent in the book is that in it authority tends to recede into the past rather than to exist in the present. The prophets introduced their message with the words "Thus says Yahweh (now)," whereas the priests teaching was in the terms of "This is what the Law (i. e. mishpat or custom) says (in the past)."

F. The Teaching of Deuteronomy.

1. Duty towards God. The Shema (Deuteronomy 6:4,5) is the basic confession of Judaism. "Hear O Israel: The Lord our God is one Lord; and you shall love the Lord your God with all your heart, and with all your soul, and with all your might." In these verses *heart* means intelligence, *soul* means life, and *might* means power. Deuteronomy says that Yahweh has chosen Israel (Chaps. 6,8) not because it was good, but because he loved it. He

is not capricious but is morally dependable. The worship of him is required of every Hebrew. The Book is a call to love, gratitude, faith, and obedience. The way to please God is not by sacrifice, but by obedience (Cf. Deut. 26:17ff.).

2. Duty towards neighbor. Deuteronomy emphasizes the fact that the content of God's command goes far beyond a centralized worship at Jerusalem. Worship is a means to a certain kind and quality of life. Life itself is meant to be humane and directed towards one's neighbor. The social emphasis in Deuteronomy is stronger than the cultic interest.

One specific way that this idea was implemented was through the establishment of cities of refuge. In order to provide for the security of those who should accidentally kill a man, six cities[2] were established as cities of refuge so that the slayer might go there and have time to prepare his defense before the judges. Otherwise the kinsmen of the deceased had the right to extract revenge by killing the slayer. Three of these cities were established on each side of the Jordan: Kedesh, Hebron, and Shechem on the west, Bezer, Golan, and Ramoth-Gilead on the east.[3] These cities were to have an easy access by means of good, well-marked roads. If the manslayer was found innocent by the judges in the city, he was allowed to live in safety within the city to which he had fled. Otherwise he would be put to death. Even though he was found innocent, he was not free to leave the city until the death of the local high-priest.

In addition to this concern about the protection of accidental slayers, there was a concern for the poor. They were to be paid daily, they were to enjoy festivals as well as the rich, the gleanings in the fields were to be left for them, they were allowed to pluck grapes and grain if this food were eaten on the spot, an upper millstone (a necessity in preparation of flour and meal) was not to be taken as security for a loan, nor were garments taken in pledge (i. e., as a token of indebtedness) to be kept overnight.

There was concern over the treatment of captives, women, slaves, and animals. Laws were passed against moving boundary stones, concerning the return of lost articles, the waging of a "just" war.[4]

All of these concerns for the maintenance of justice and the preservation of dignity represent a new and important dimension in Hebrew culture.

G. A Philosophy of History.

Deuteronomy not only expresses a firm conviction that justice ought to be practiced within Judaism, but also that the concept of justice is an inescapable law of history. Goodness will be rewarded and evil will be punished. In fact, the Deuteronomic historians read this idea back into the whole past of Israel. Those who are faithful to Yahweh prosper, those who are not come to grief. The Deuteronomist believed there were many motives for men's actions. Among them were the desire for reward, the fear of punishment, as well as gratitude, humility, and loyalty to Yahweh. No notice is taken yet of the fact that obedience does not always precede a reward and that it is not only the sinners who suffer.

[1] cf. 2 Chronicles 34 for the story of the finding of the book.
[2] cf. Numbers 35:6.
[3] cf. Joshua 20:7, 8.
[4] cf. Deuteronomy 20.

Chapter XX

JEREMIAH, EZEKIEL, II ISAIAH.

A. Jeremiah.

Jeremiah, a citizen of Judah, was born c. 645 B. C. in Anathoth, a small town about five miles northeast of Jerusalem. Jeremiah was a man of property, of a relatively high social status, respected in the community, learned, and unmarried. This combination was unusual for a Hebrew in the 7th century B. C.

In 626 B. C. ("In the thirteenth year of the reign of Josiah") he began to preach – i. e. to prophesy. The dates of his ministry, or prophesying activity, were between 626 and 580 B. C. In those years the Scythians invaded Palestine,[1] and Nineveh, the capitol of Assyria, fell to the combined forces of the Babylonians, Medes, and Scythians (612 B. C.). King Josiah, the leader of the great reform in Israel, was killed at the Battle of Megiddo in 609 B. C. The Babylonians won a decisive victory over the Assyrians and Egyptians at the Battle of Carchemish in 605 B. C. Jehoiakim, a vassal appointed by Pharaoh Neccho, ruled Judah between 608 and 598 B. C. However, upon Neccho's defeat in 605 at Carchemish, Jehoiakim switched his allegiance to Nebuchadnezzar, King of Babylon. In 597 B. C. Jerusalem was taken by the Babylonians, and many of its leading citizens were deported to

Babylon, but the city was spared. Zedekiah, a weak king, governed Judah from 597 to 586 B. C. In 586 B. C. Jerusalem was captured by the Babylonians and razed. The remainder of its inhabitants were exported to Babylon.

B. Why is Jeremiah Important Today?

There are several reasons why the Book of Jeremiah is relevant to the modern reader. If we are living at the end of an era (and it is becoming increasingly clear that we are), then Jeremiah can interpret the meaning and significance of such a time for us, since he lived at the end of the era of the existence of Judah.

Furthermore he has something worthwhile to say to those who are persecuted for conscience's sake. Many people in the twentieth century have been persecuted for their conscientious views about war, the draft, and civil rights.

Jeremiah was the first to emphasize the importance of inner motives and convictions. He believed that a right relationship between man and God must also exist on an emotional level, in a man's heart. This reflects the importance that psychiatrists place on an inner unity of the drives of psychic energy which appear as reason, emotion, and intuition. For these reasons Jeremiah can be regarded as a "modern man" with something relevant to say.

C. Jeremiah's Teaching.

Although his general moral and religious teaching denounce the same evils as his predecessors, he represents an advance over them in that he identified himself with the people, and within that identification spoke with compassion to them (cf. 8:18ff.). This kind of sentiment was never expressed by Amos, Hosea, or Isaiah.

Jeremiah saw clearly that sin was not only corrosive of character, but was habit forming. He asks, "Can the Ethiopian change his skin or the leopard his spots? Then also you can do good who are accustomed to do evil" (13:23).

The complacency of the Hebrews was attacked by Jeremiah. They felt that since they had the Temple and the holy city Jerusalem, their religious (and hence their political) problems were automatically solved. The prophet saw that Yahweh pays attention to attitudes and motives, not to religious equipment.

Thus says the Lord: "Let not the wise man

> glory in his wisdom, let not the mighty man glory in his might, let not the rich man glory in his riches; but let him who glories glory in this, that he understands and knows me, that I am the Lord who practices steadfast love, justice, and righteousness in the earth; for in these things I delight, says the Lord."
>
> 9:23,24

Jeremiah's teaching dealt specifically with his own situation. He did not resort to platitudes or generalities. He dealt with the particulars of slaves, resistance to the enemy, surrender, the ownership of private property, etc. Essentially he was an advocate of the *status quo,* urging Judah to submit to Babylon and not to revolt. In all these convictions he said what he thought was true, even though it offended those who heard it. He did not care about his own popularity, and thus paid a high price for independence and integrity. The cost was loneliness, ostracism, and imprisonment.

Jeremiah is sometimes called "The Father of Prayer." Prayer for him was not a mechanical observance, but a sincere and living encounter with Yahweh. He opened his heart and spoke his mind to God. He had enough familiarity with God to condemn his own enemies. Yet he was aware of the possibility of self-deception. He was as honest with himself as he could be, never afraid to admit that he could have been wrong. All these attributes and teachings were directed at the establishment of the worth of the individual. Hence the human situation is seen in a new light. In this light even suffering takes on a new meaning – it holds the possiblity of a greater good.

The climax of the Book is found in Jeremiah 31:31 – 33.

> Behold, the days are coming, says the Lord, when I will make a new covenant with the house of Israel and the house of Judah, not like the covenant which I made with their fathers when I took them by the hand to bring them out of the land of Egypt, my covenant which they broke, though I was their husband, says the Lord. But this is the covenant which I will make with the house of

> Israel after those days, says the Lord; I will put my law within them, and I will write it upon their hearts; and I will be their God, and they shall be my people.

This is the New Covenant on which the New Testament is built. It is a covenant of the spirit.

D. Ezekiel. Sixth Century Background.

There were two deportations from Jerusalem to Babylon, one in 597 B. C. and one in 586 B. C. Ezekiel was among the first exiles, and began to preach in Babylon in 592 B. C. (the 5th year of king Jehoiakim's captivity, and the 30th year after the publication of Deuteronomy).[2] In 586 B. C. the Hebrews were divided into three parts. There were probably about 20,000 deportees to Babylon. This was the cream of the population: artisans, intellectuals, Temple servants, etc. Some Hebrews went to Egypt. Jeremiah was with this group. The majority stayed in Palestine. They had a difficult time agriculturally.

Those who were deported to Babylon found themselves in a large city, at the center of a sophisticated culture, given relative freedom in matters of living quarters, choice of occupation and practice of religion. In this atmosphere, the exclusivism of the Hebrews, which in the past had kept them from contamination by the influence of surrounding nations, was difficult to maintain. Temple worship was no longer possible, and the tradition that it grew out of was in danger of becoming forgotten and lost.

Ezekiel's clearcut purpose was to retain the tradition and to keep the Covenant relationship alive.[3] The loss of the Temple and the preservation of tradition by means of worship there, was compensated for by the establishment of synagogues, where the concepts of Judaism were taught, and by a rise in importance of the Law as a fixed guide to maintenance of *mishpat*.

E. The Teaching of Ezekiel.

The Hebrews in exile asked, "Why has this disaster come to Israel?" Ezekiel implied that it was because the inhabitants of Jerusalem were unfaithful to Yahweh. In chapters 8 and 9 he describes in mystical terms the glory of God leaving the Temple in gradual stages.

It has been pointed out that one of the credentials of a prophet is a "call." Ezekiel's call is in the form of a vision of Yahweh which is found in Chapter 1. This is a mystical description of Yahweh, filled with symbolism. Yahweh is in the storm cloud – a classical expression stemming back to Sinai. The appearance of the figures – lion, ox, eagle, and man – show the influence of Babylonian sculpture. The wheels represent the omnipresence of God, while the eyes represent his omniscience. Chapter 1, verse 23 ("And under the firmament their wings were stretched out straight, one toward another") may reflect the mercy seat in the Temple. In any event, Ezekiel's description of Yahweh shows a synthesis of the art and ideas of two cultures – the Hebrew and the Babylonian. The memory of the nature of Yahweh is being kept alive through the use of Babylonian patterns and thought forms.

Another distinct and unique facet of Ezekiel's teaching is the conviction that each person has a responsibility to keep himself morally straight. The effects of environment and heredity are minimized. The old philosophy was, "The fathers have eaten sour grapes and the children's teeth are set on edge." Now there is a different emphasis:

> As I live, says the Lord God, this proverb (about sour grapes) shall no more be used by you in Israel. Behold, all souls are mine; the soul of the father as well as the soul of the son is mine; the soul that sins shall die.
> 18:4

Among the exiles the question also arose, "In view of the disaster of the collapse of Judah, does Yahweh still care?" Ezekiel says that he does, and gives as a kind of parable about this a story about the denunciation of shepherds who feed on their own sheep (cf. 34:1 – 11).

This same theme is further developed in the description of the Valley of Dry Bones (Ezekiel 37). Even though Israel as a nation is dead, and even though she has been scattered – Israel by Assyria and Judah by Babylonia – God will reunite the people and restore the nation to life.

Ezekiel believes that after the Exile, a New Commonwealth will emerge. There will be a New Temple, a new social order, a new spirit in the resurrected nation (cf. Ezekiel 40 – 48).

F. II Isaiah (Isaiah 40 – 66)

These chapters of Isaiah were written in the 6th and 5th centuries B. C. and assembled by an editor c. 400 B. C. or later. There is a marked contrast in the emphases between I and II Isaiah. The differences are as follows:

I Isaiah	II Isaiah
1. Punishment of Israel and Judah is threatened.	1. The punishment has been inflicted.
2. The Hebrews are rebuked.	2. The Hebrews are encouraged.
3. Emphasis is on repentance for past sins.	3. Belief is in hope for the future.
4. The dominant power is Assyria.	4. The dominant power is Babylonia and Persia.
5. Spoken preaching.	5. Written theology.

II Isaiah answers four fundamental questions. They are as follows:

1. What is God like?

Here is the first fully developed expression of monotheism – a picture of a saving, loving, forgiving God. Up to this time the Hebrews believed that they had an obligation to worship only Yahweh, but they did not deny the reality of the existence of other gods (for example, the baals). Now they come to the conclusion that there is only one purpose in history. God is both creator and redeemer.

> Turn to me and be saved, all the ends of the earth!
> For I am God, and there is no other!
>
> Isaiah 45:22

This is one of the great climaxes of the Old Testament. In support of this idea, but in a negative way, idols are mocked. For the most sarcastic and ironic treatment of this theme read Isaiah 44:12 ff.

2. What is Man's duty to man?

II Isaiah develops the theme that Israel has a missionary duty to carry the knowledge of Yahweh to the ends of the earth. "I will give you as a light to the nations, that my salvation may reach to the ends of the earth" (49:6b). This means that there is a doctrine of God in relationship to man. God reveals himself as always working on man's behalf. Although man is finite and sinful, he has the power to be included in God's work. This theme is treated with humor and good effect in the Book of Jonah.

3. What is the work and character of the Suffering Servant?

The description of the Suffering Servant is found in four separate segments of II Isaiah as follows:

42:1-4
49:1-6
50:4-11
52:13-53: 12

These four poems were originally a single literary unit taken from some other work and embedded in II Isaiah. They all have the same metre. There is no clue concerning their date or place or origin.

The Servant is described in various ways which reflect the Hebrew capacity for thought in corporate terms.[4] In 42:1-13 the servant is an amalgam of an individual and the Hebrew nation.

In 49:1 – 6 he is three things: an individual, all of Israel, part of Israel. He is simply an individual in 50:4 – 11. In 52:13 – 53:12 he is once more an amalgam of an individual and the nation.

This poem (or these poems) expresses a new idea as far as Israel's role in history goes. It contains the seeds of the idea that God's Messiah will suffer on behalf of others. This is called vicarious suffering. It resolves itself in some good result which overcomes the evil of suffering. Israel's task is to become God's servant and its goal is to bring all mankind to an understanding of Him. This concept was central to Jesus' ideas about his own identity and ministry.

4. What is the spirit in which to approach God?

Isaiah's answer is essentially a spirit of penitence and fasting. This is perfectly summed up in Chapter 58, which is to be read at this point as the basic answer to the fourth question.

In summary, these three prophets – Jeremiah, Ezekiel, and II Isaiah – represent the basic concerns of the Hebrews immediately before, during, and immediately after the Babylonian Exile. This is a period of transition in which the expression of the relationship between Yahweh and nation goes from Temple worship and prophecy to an emphasis on the importance of Law and the priesthood within the establishment of the synagogue as an institution.

[1] cf. page 84

[2] cf. Ezekiel 1:1, 2.

[3] The nature of the problem is seen in a letter written by Jeremiah to the exiles. Cf. Jer. 29.

[4] cf. page 82.

Chapter XXI

WISDOM LITERATURE

A. Historical Background.

The three basic examples of Wisdom Literature are the books of Proverbs, Ecclesiastes, and Job. These writings are the beginning of a bridge between the Old and New Testaments. They were written in the late Persian, the Greek, and the Roman Periods (4th to 2nd centuries B. C.). They represent the response of the Hebrews to Hellenistic ideas which were bursting in from the surrounding world. Wisdom Literature bridges Law and Prophesy. The prophets emphasized the transcendence of Yahweh at the expense of his immanence. The prophets' demands to oppose idolatry, to love God, and to respect one's neighbor, often placed too heavy a burden on the common man. The priests, on the other hand, emphasized the immanence of Yahweh. For them *this* world is good; the Law is to be done here. God is at work within the material order.

Wisdom Literature tried to bridge this immanence and transcendence of God, to mediate between God and his world. The most common phrase used to express this mediation is "The Word of God" – a personal creative agent, concrete and efficacious. The human word can bless or curse, but the Word of God was taken by the Hebrews to be an agent of creation.[1]

B. Defects of Wisdom Literature.

Wisdom Literature lacks the force of mythological and prophetic writings because of a shift of interest from God to man, or from man in general to oneself. There is an increase in humanistic behavior with an emphasis on what is good for society and the self. Personal virtues are stressed, often to the exclusion of Yahweh. The Proverbs are prudential advice, but lack the authority of the word of God. The contents of Job emphasize speculation about God rather than word from him. In all these writings morality is prudential, based on the question, "What is best for me?" The emphasis on self-sacrifice and forgiveness has been lost. There is too much desire for respectability accompanied by the belief that righteousness can be acquired by keeping the commandments and acting prudently.

C. Job as Wisdom Literature.

The author of the Book of Job is sometimes called the Shakespeare of the Bible. It contains the most learned writing in the Old Testament – perhaps the greatest writing before Plato. The book is commonly supposed to deal with the problem "Why does a good God with power permit a good man to suffer beyond the limits of fairness?" Why is suffering out of proportion to sin? Perhaps there is another question beneath the surface. Does Job undergo his suffering unless he feels that ultimately God will reward him?

The basis of the essential question of Job is the Deuteronomic doctrine that the good are rewarded and the evil punished, sharpened in accordance with Ezekiel 18:4, "The soul that sins, *it* shall die".

It is not easy to determine what the Book of Job is trying to say. One possibility is that Yahweh is unrighteous. Cf. Job 9:20 – 22.

> "Though I am innocent, my own mouth would condemn me;
> though I am blameless, he would prove me perverse.
> I am blameless; I regard not myself; I loathe my life.
> It is all one; therefore I say, he destroys both the blameless and
> the wicked."

Or is the book saying that Job is really a sinner in spite of all his protests (his chief sin being his pride)? Or is the book saying that God is incomprehensible? If so, to argue with God is futile, hence the answer to suffering is in the realm of faith rather than the intellect.

Another possible answer to the dilemma is that Job will ultimately be rewarded if he is faithful. Lastly the book may be trying to say that man must keep searching for God's ways unfathomable as they seem.

The text of Job itself represents a collation of many sources. It is beyond our purpose to separate them; it is only necessary to point out that each of the authors really gives up the problem of the source of suffering. The prose framework gives up the problem by saying that Job is ultimately rewarded. In 42:10 the Lord restores the fortunes of Job. The question of his earlier family that was destroyed (Job 1) is left unanswered.

The speeches of Yahweh (Job 38, 39) give up the problem by saying that a man ought to trust God for he cannot understand him anyway.

Job's so-called "comforters" maintain the orthodox position that calamity is retribution for sin. God is in fact lenient, they say, and we should be led to repent. Eliphaz, the first of Job's friends suggests that there is disciplinary value in suffering. Bildad, the second friend, maintains that the wisdom of the ancients tells us that God gives man his just due. Zophar, the last comforter suggests to Job that God is lenient, and that he is really getting off lightly. None of these answers is very satisfying. In addition, if we take them at face value, it makes Job a liar since he vigorously defends his innocence (Job 31).

The book itself seems to support Job's innocence, and stands behind his audacity in speaking freely, even to Yahweh. It is an appeal for total honesty rather than morbid, self-effacing confession. It shows a preference for raising the difficult problems and struggling with them, rather than accepting over-simplified dogmatic answers – such as the belief that the good are rewarded and the evil suffer. As did Jeremiah, Job clings to God, his final court of appeal: "Behold, he will slay me; I have no hope; yet I will defend my ways to his face" (13:15), or "For I know that my Redeemer lives, and at last he will stand upon the earth" (19:25).

Some Other Answers to the Problem of Suffering.

In Apocalyptic Literature, i. e. literature about the end of the age, and a future life, the problem is solved by putting off the rewards into the Age to Come. In the Psalms the answer is trust.

God, who has been found faithful in this life, will not abandon his creatures in the future. The Suffering Servant poems in Isaiah imply that suffering may be vicariously redemptive. Although one person suffers, others may benefit from it. The Christian position is that a great deal of suffering is due to *man's* sin, and in the life, death, and resurrection of Jesus, God has acted to save man from man's own folly.

There are several other Old Testament passages that raise this problem. They are as follows:

1. Daniel 9. We have not obeyed God, and suffering is the result.
2. Jeremiah 12. "Why does the way of the wicked prosper?"
3. Ezekiel 18. "The fathers have eaten sour grapes and the children's teeth are set on edge."
4. Habakkuk 1:13. "Thou who art of purer eyes than to behold evil and canst not look on wrong, why dost thou look on faithless men, and art silent when the wicked swallows up the man more righteous than he?"
5. Genesis 50:20. "As for you, you meant evil against me; but God meant it for good, to bring it about that many people should be kept alive, as they are today."
6. Exodus 20:5ff. ". . . for I the Lord your God am a jealous God, visiting the iniquities of the fathers upon the children to the third and fourth generation of those who hate me, but showing steadfast love to thousands of those who love me and keep my commandments."
7. Isaiah 63:8, 9. "For he (the Lord) said, Surely they (the Hebrews) are my people, sons who will not deal falsely; and he became their Savior. In all their affliction he was afflicted, and the angel of his presence saved them; in his love and in his pity he redeemed them; he lifted them up and carried them all the days of old."
8. Isaiah 21:21 ff. "On that day the Lord will punish the host of heaven, in heaven and the kings of the earth, on the earth. They will be gathered together as prisoners in a pit; they will be shut up in a prison, and after many days they will be punished."
9. That whole book of Ecclesiastes says that nothing can be done about evil

10. The Deuteronomist (D) says that the good will be rewarded and the evil punished.

E. Proverbs.

375 Proverbs are attributed to Solomon. This is because in the Hebrew system of counting, each letter stands for a number.

If one adds the numbers which are equivalents to the letters in the word "Solomon", the sum is 375. However, since the outlook of the book is monotheistic, they cannot be attributed to Solomon, but rather to some date between 400 and 200 B. C. Proverbs 21:9, "It is better to live in a corner of the housetop than in a house shared with a contentious woman", is hardly likely to have been the sentiment of a king who spent 13 years building his palace and had a retinue of 1000 wives and concubines.

Some of the Proverbs have a kind of humanistic merit, e. g.: "Better is a dinner of herbs where love is than a fatted ox and hatred with it" (15:17), or "pride goes before destruction, and a haughty spirit before a fall" (16:18), or "Train up a child in the way he should go, and when he is old he will not depart from it." (22:6). However, they generally comprise a prudential ethic whose aim is happiness. The compiler deals with manners, morals, conduct, and human relations. All of life is within the range of his interest. The sayings are mostly personal and rather selfish. They hold no high ideal. They direct man's attention away from God and neighbor towards himself.

F. Summary.

With the Babylonian exile, the political history of Israel came to a close. Wisdom Literature reflects this change. The Hebrew came to see himself, not as part of a political system, but as an individual who found his orientation in a personal reaction to everyday life. The basis for this orientation was a concept of wisdom as reasonableness, or a knowledge of one's limitations.

The question then became, "Where is wisdom to be found?" (Job 28). The answer was, "Yahweh understands the way of it, and knows its place" (Job 28:23). A relationship between Yahweh and wisdom was created, and wisdom become personified.[2] She is created by Yahweh (Proverbs 8:22-30).

Wisdom became the means through which Yahweh related himself to human beings. Ultimately, the earlier biblical material – the patriarchal histories, the Law, and the Prophets – came to be read as Wisdom literature. It had worth because it was wise, or reflected wisdom

With some notable exceptions (e. g. Maccabees), the writings of Judaism after 587 B. C. reflect a continuing separation of history and religion. There was no longer any possibility of an Israel whose empirical history could be the medium of Yahweh's revelation to the world. The Wisdom idiom became the lasting statement upon which Rabbinic Judaism was (and is) based.

[1] "In the beginning was the Word, and the Word was with God . . . . all things were made through him". John 1:1 – 3.

'And God said (i. e. spoke the Word), "Let there be a firmament . . ."' Gen. 1:6.

"By the word of the Lord the heavens were made." Psalm 33:6.

[2] And is sometimes feminine in gender. C. f. Proverbs 7:4; 8:1,2.

Chapter XXII

THE PSALMS.

A. Origin and Development of the Psalms.

Even though the name which is most closely associated with the Psalms is that of King David, he was not the author of any of them. They are chiefly the praises of Israel, the Temple hymns. They come to us today through the synagogues and the Christian church. Even as hymns change in character – for example from Gregorian chant, to simple two part music, to Bach's chorales, to Puritan hymns, to Victorian hymns, to the jazz mass – so did the Psalms change in character and style. They come out of the common life of Israel. They are the end product of a long sifting process; a deposit of many years of corporate living. They contain no daring thought, no heresy, no audacity. They are of humble origin, close to the common life of the common man. They speak to all because they sprang from the life of all. However, their impact in the twentieth century has been almost completely nullified since they come to us in the grammatical forms of Elizabethan English. If the original force of their language and thought could be restored, we would see again their powerful portrayal of life in imagery and metaphor.

To some extent the Psalms were influenced by the literature of other nations. For example Psalm 104 is similar to Akneton's *Hymn to the Sun.* Psalm 19 is similar to the Assyrian hymn to the sun god Shamash.

Five types of psalms are discernible:

1. Songs of praise (hymns)
2. Communal laments
3. Royal psalms
4. Individual laments
5. Individual thanksgivings

Most of the psalms were written between 450 and 250 B. C., although some were written as late as 50 B. C.

B. Form of the Psalms.

Psalms were written in poetic lines. For the Hebrew the essence of poetry was rhythm. Rhyme was not a factor. Therefore Hebrew poetry consisted of series of accents, with the accents forming the time intervals. Usual rhythms are 4-4, 4-3, or 2-2. This poetry was generally not written in stanzas, but rather in 8, 20, 30, 40, 50, 70, or 100 line poems. Other poems have 22 lines – or multiples of 22 – since there were 22 letters in the Hebrew alphabet. This lent itself to the use of an acrostic, where every line began with a successive letter of the Hebrew alphabet.

About one quarter of the psalter is made up of eight line poems because a scroll was eight lines wide.

C. Defects and Strengths.

The psalms are weak in many ways in spite of their greatness. They contain curses upon foreign nations in contrast to a strong expression of nationalism towards the Hebrews. They retain the Deuteronomic belief that good is always rewarded and evil punished. They are often self-righteous. For the psalmist, as for every Hebrew, death is the end of all, there is no hope of eternal life. Many psalms are difficult to interpret. They reflect a preoccupation with the idea that the Hebrews have been unduly persecuted.

Opposed to this, however, is the content which has made the psalms great as a body of literature. They express a strong feeling of trust as the proper response to God. The elements of thanksgiving and praise are beautifully expressed. Sixty-five psalms contain a feeling of love for the community which is the beginning of one of the requirements for a civilized life. The psalms refer to the God of history rather than the less sophisticated idea of the God of nature.

D. Themes of the Psalms.

There are many basic themes expressed in the psalms. The major ones are as follows:

1. A Doctrine of God.
   a. God is eternal. Cf. Psalm 90 – "For a thousand years in thy sight are but as yesterday when it is past, or as a watch in the night."
   b. God is the eternal creator. Cf. Psalm 102 – "Of old thou didst lay the foundation of the earth, and the heavens are the work of thy hands. They will perish, but thou dost endure; they will all wear out like a garment."
   c. The universe reflects the majesty of God. Cf. Psalm 104 – "Thou art clothed with honor and majesty, who coverest thyself with light as with a garment, who hast stretched out the heavens like a tent.
   d. All creatures are subject to God. Cf. Psalm 145 – "The eyes of all look to thee, and thou givest them their food in due season."
2. The Character of God.
   a. God is a savior. Cf. Psalm 103 – "Bless the Lord, O my soul; and all that is within me, bless his holy name! Bless the Lord, O my soul, and forget not all his benefits, who forgives all your iniquity, who heals all your diseases, who redeems your life from the Pit, who crowns you with steadfast love and mercy."
   b. The first great presupposition of the psalms is that God shows *hesed* (steadfast love).
   c. God reveals himself most clearly through his dealings with men in history. Cf. Psalm 114 – "When Israel went forth from Egypt, the house of Jacob from a people of strange language, Judah became his sanctuary, Israel his dominion." and cf. Psalm 82 – "God has taken his place in the divine council; in the midst of the rulers of earthly nations he holds judgment."
3. A Doctrine of Man.
   a. God is always ready to help man, but man sacrifices to

God with the wrong motive. When he does sacrifice, it is too formal, and often he fails to ask God for help. Cf. Psalm 50 –

"If I were hungry, I would not tell you,
for the world and all that is in it is mine.
Do I eat of the flesh of bulls, or drink the
blood of goats?
Offer to God a sacrifice of thanksgiving,
and pay your vows to the Most High;
and call upon me in the day of trouble;
I will deliver you, and you shall glorify me."

b. Man should realize the need for penance. Cf. Psalm 51 –

"Create in me a clean heart, O God,
and put a new and right spirit within me.
Cast me not away from thy presence,
and take not thy holy Spirit from me."

4. The Law. Not many psalms directly mention the Law. In the psalms the law is not one of casuistry or ceremony, but a law which is derived from the love of God and which issues from doing his will in the moral sphere. The practices of Judaism and formalism are condemned. Cf. Psalm 1 – "Blessed is the man who walks not in the counsel of the wicked, nor stands in the way of sinners, nor sits in the seat of scoffers; but his delight is in the law of the Lord, and on his law he meditates day and night."
and Psalm 119 – "Blessed are those whose way is blameless, who walk in the law of the Lord!"
and Psalm 40 – "Burnt offering and sin offering thou hast not required."

5. The Temple. Mention of the Temple appears in 65 psalms. There is a recognition of a connection between spiritual religion and material institutions. The essence of the revelation of God in the Judaeo-Christian heritage is that God is revealed through material things and in history. The Temple was considered to be the focal point of God's revelation to man, the place of his most precious memories. History is centered here. God's house and the community's house is a corrective to individual selfish religion. It is a place of memory and hope.

a. Cf. Psalm 42 – "As a hart longs for flowing streams, so longs my soul for thee, O God. My soul thirsts for God, for the living God. When shall I come and behold the face of God?"

b. Psalm 43 – "Oh send out thy light and they truth; let them lead me, let them bring me to thy holy hill and to thy dwelling."

c. Psalm 48 – "His holy mountain, beautiful in elevation, is the joy of all the earth, Mount Zion in the far north."

d. Psalm 122 – "I was glad when they said to me, 'Let us go to the house of the Lord!' "

6. The Kingdom. Psalm 82 contains a picture of God's rule. The kings of the earth are called to judgment. Justice will establish them. God controls history and sifts the nations. God's concern for the poor and meek is expressed. He cares about righteousness among men, dealings with one's neighbor. He is opposed to pride and arrogance. The psalm provides us with some picture of the kingdom which is to. Also see:

a. Psalm 72 – "Let the mountains bear prosperity for the people, and the hills, in righteousness!"

b. Psalm 50 – "Out of Zion, the perfection of beauty, God shines forth."

c. Psalm 146 – "The Lord watches over the sojourners, he upholds the widow and the fatherless; but the way of the wicked he brings to ruin."

7. Trust. The names that the Psalms give to God are indicative of trust, e. g., rock, fortress, shield, support, light, salvation, hope, confidence, helper, savior.

a. Psalm 4 – "In peace I will both lie down and sleep; for thou alone, O Lord, makest me dwell in safety."

b. Psalm 23 – "Even though I walk through the valley of the shadow of death, I fear no evil."

c. Psalm 27 – "For my father and my mother have forsaken me, but the Lord will take me up."

d. Psalm 31 – "In thee O Lord, do I seek refuge; Let me never be put to shame."

e. Psalm 139 – "Thou searchest out my path and my lying down, and art acquainted with all my ways."

8. Suffering. The answer of the Psalmist to suffering is not an explanation of where it comes from, but rather a response in trust that is better than an explanation. Ninety Psalms deal with adversity. The Psalmist cries for help and is

always delivered. He finds a rock on which to put his feet and finds joys even in the midst of suffering. The orthodox view of the Deuteronomist supposes a close connection between sin and suffering but this view doesn't dominate the psalter even though it is present (The orthodox view is found in Psalms I and 91).

a. Psalm 17. There is a view that suffering is a test.
"If thou triest my heart, if thou visitest me
by night, if thou tested me, thou wilt
find no wickedness in me."

b. Psalm 71. There is a view that suffering is a discipline.
"Thou who hast made me see many sore
troubles wilt revive me again."
There is no doctrine of vicarious suffering in the psalms. There is some indication that suffering is an unfathomable mystery. The best statement is found in Psalm 73:2 – 16.

9. Future Life.

The greater part of the Old Testament says that death is the end – no part of man worthy of reverence or importance survives. Immortality was associated with pagan gods and the death and resurrection cycle of nature. It was only in the latest days of Judaism (3rd century B. C.) under the influence of Hellenistic thought that the individual assumed any importance. There was some belief in a shadowy life in Sheol after death.

Psalm 116:15 – "Precious in the sight of the Lord is the death of his saints."

Psalm 8 – "What is man that thou are mindful of him. and the son of man that thou
dost care for him?
Yet thou hast made him
little less than God,
and dost crown him with glory
and honor."

Key to Passages Cited

1:1,2	71:20
4:8	72:3
8:4,5	82:1
17:3	90:4

23:10
31:1
40:6b
42:1,2
43:3
48:1a-2b
50:2
50:12,15
51:10,11

102:25,26
103:1-4
104:1b-2
114:1
116:15
119:1
122:1
139:3
145:15
146:9

Chapter XXIII

Apocalyptic Literature.
The End of the Old Covenant and the Beginning of the New.

A. Introduction.

Apocalyptic literature deals in specific terms with the doctrine of last things, or the end of history. Eschatology is the treatment of this subject in general terms. Apocalyptic literature is an attempt to escape from the specific problems of the present into the future. Examples of Apocalyptic literature are:

Daniel
Joel
Isaiah 24 – 27
Zechariah 9 – 14
Ezekiel 38, 39
Obadiah
Isaiah 11:1 – 9
Jeremiah 23:5 – 8

The dates of these writings extend from 200 B. C. to 100 A. D.; however, most of them can be dated between 50 B. C. and 30 A. D. The Hebrews lost interest in the subject when the Christians became involved in it.

Apocalyptic literature is an outgrowth of prophecy. The

prophets had already mentioned "The Day of the Lord." The day never arrived. When the writing of prophetic literature faded away, it was replaced by Apocalyptic literature and the prophets fell into temporary disrepute.[1] Whereas prophetic writing was realistic, apocalypticism was a literature of escape. The prophets stayed within a naturalistic framework for the most part, but miracles abound in writings about the last days. The style of the prophets was restrained. The apocalypticists wrote in a fantastic and obscure way. For the prophet, present history was of crucial importance; this was replaced by the idea that only the end of history was important. The doom of the prophets gave way to hope. Judgment now was transposed to judgment at the end of the age. The prophets saw foreign nations as the tools of God's punishment, but in apocalyptic literature foreign nations are the victims of the wrath of God. The prophets conveyed their message by the spoken word. Apocalyptic literature was written at its inception. Authorship of the prophets is certain, but we don't know who wrote books such as Daniel, Joel, and Obadiah.

B. Historical Background to Apocalyptic Literature.

The westward expansion of the Persian Empire was stopped by the Greeks in the 4th century B. C. Subsequent Greek victories brought the Mediterranean world under the influence of Alexander the Great by 326 B. C. A movement to Hellenize the world followed. This was remarkably successful. The ideas and language of the Mediterranean basin became Greek in essence.

Alexander died in 323 B. C. and the Empire was split in three parts among his generals. Egypt with its capital at Alexandria was ruled by the Ptolemies. Mesopotamia and Syria were governed by the Seleucids, with their capital at Antioch. Macedonia was ruled by the Antigonids. Events developed as follows:

1. Palestine was first ruled by the Ptolemies. This was a lenient rule. Hellenism was not an irritant to the Hebrews, except for one militant sect called the Hasidim (the pious ones).
2. In 223 B. C. Antiochus III (The Great) came to the Seleucid throne in Antioch. In 198 B. C. he won a military victory over Ptolemy V, thus conquering Palestine.
3. Antiochus IV Epihanes (175 B. C. – 163 B. C.) was one of Antiochus the Great's successors. He was a militant

Hellenizer, declaring himself to be a god. Worship of Zeus was required of the Hebrews. Antiochus IV auctioned the office of the Jewish high priest to the highest bidder. He put down a popular revolt, plundered the Temple in Jerusalem, outlawed Judaism, ordered the Torah (Jewish Law) to be burned, made the observance of the Sabbath a capital offense, desecrated the Temple by erecting an altar to Zeus over the high altar of the Hebrew priests. Pigs were sacrificed in the Temple and the Jews forced to eat them against the dietary laws. This was in 168 B. C.

4. At Modien, a Hebrew village, Mattathias the village priest revolted against Antiochus. In 166 B. C. he organized a guerilla band and bestowed the leadership of it to his son Judas, who became known as Judas Maccabeus (the Hammerer). The revolt was successful and in 165 B. C. the Temple was cleansed and restored.
5. The Maccabees ruled over the Hebrews in Palestine from 165 B. C. to 63 B. C., when Rome sent Pompey to settle a civil war. From that time until the collapse of Jerusalem in 70 A. D., the Hebrews lost their independence to the Romans.

C. The Distress of the Maccabean Period.

After the Maccabees had raised the hopes of the Jews to a high point, the suffering, oppression, and bad times went from bad to worse. Apocalyptic literature written during this period became a series of tracts for bad times, a literature of despair. The only way out for the Hebrews seemed to be through God's direct and immediate intervention. The apocalypticist asks, "How long will the suffering continue? Is God indifferent? Is there any sense in the world? Is there any hope beyond this life?"

D. Influence from Persia.

Features of Zoroastrianism, the religion of Persia, are found in apocalyptic literature. These include references to angels, divine retribution, judgment, a dualistic philosophy (powers in heaven in conflict with men on earth), the Messiah (a representative of God), cycles of years, ages of gold, silver, brass, and iron, and powers of light and darkness.

E. Characteristics of Apocalyptic Literature.

Apocalyptic literature has three essential characteristics, although there are many variations on these themes. They are as follows:

1. An assumption that there are two ages, the present age and the age to come. This is an essential dualism which is also reflected in other dualisms such as those of heaven and earth, light and darkness, good and evil, angels and demons, etc. There is a belief that the present age is not only bad but is getting worse, but all this will be resolved in the age to come. At that time disease, pain, sorrow, error, anguish, and death will cease to exist. The present world will dissolve in all its aspects, the mountains will melt like wax and the moon turn to blood, the stars will fall from the heavens. But this dissolution is not the end. It is a preparation for things to come. There will be a new heaven and a new earth – all things will be made new and pain and sorrow and death will be no more.
2. The new age will be brought in only by God's activity. History is leading up to this moment, but it will be preceded by worsening times.
3. God's intervention will be miraculous. It will result in the establishment of the glory of Israel, an increase in her prosperity, the slaughter of her enemies, and finally the resurrection of her martyrs.

F. Defects of Apocalyptic Literature.

Apocalyptic literature is deficient in overlooking the fact that *this* world is also God's world. He ought not to be confined to the age to come. Man should not abandon his heritage to the powers of evil, but work here and now as a co-creator with God. Apocalyptic literature places too much stress on the sinful nature of the world. An emphasis on Hebrew exclusivism is another weakness of these writings. Other nations, as well as Israel, are precious in the sight of God. There is a loss of the idea that judgment is not confined to a single day between the two ages, but is taking place at all times and in all places.

G. The Value of Apocalyptic Literature.

The emphasis of this literature is right in that it insists that

God is in control and is taking the initiative in the process of redemption. It sees that man cannot solve his problems by himself. There is no inevitable progress. History is coming to a purposive end. Apocalyptic literature holds out hope for another and a better world. Man is created for a destiny that he has not yet discovered.

These writings provide a sense of urgency which is not equally true of any of the other frameworks of history. The Greeks saw themselves separated from the perfect world by space. The classical Hebrews were separated from the perfect world by time, but apocalyptic writing brings home the idea that the Kingdom of God is near at hand, and man must be ready for it.

H. The Book of Daniel.

The Book of Daniel is divided into two parts, viz., chapters 1 through 6 and chapters 7 through 12. The first part contains six stories that illustrate God's care for those who support him unconditionally. The last seven chapters contain descriptions of four visions.

Some points that come out of the stories and visions are as follows:

1. Young Jews in Babylon thrive on vegetables. This is saying that their welfare comes about not through what they eat but through obedience to Yahweh.
2. David's interpretation of Nebuchadnezzar's dream concerning an idol made of gold, silver, bronze, iron, and clay is saying that the world is running downhill. This has been alluded to above as one typical aspect of apocalyptic writing.
3. In the story of Shadrach, Meshach, and Abednego, a fourth man appears in the fire. This is to illustrate God's presence with his servants in time of trial.
4. In the tree-vision, God orders the tree cut down. This alludes to a rebuke of Nebuchadnezzar's pride (Belteshazzar is another name for Daniel).

The purpose of the Book of Daniel is to encourage the Jews in Maccabean times by citing examples of trust and deliverance. Yahweh takes care of his people by promoting their faith. The book was written in a time of great persecution when the Seleucids were being driven from Jerusalem in 165 B. C. (even though it purports to have been written in the 6th century B. C.).

I. General Conclusion.

We have come a long way from the analysis of the myths and legends in Genesis. We have surveyed 2000 years of the history of the Hebrew race and 1000 years of its literature. This is a people who were convinced that they had a unique experience of the one true God whom they knew as Yahweh. They believed that he was at work in and through the history of other nations. Perhaps they would not have denied that other nations had some distorted glimpse of him through their own gods – just as the Hebrews first knew him under the forms of the local gods of Mesopotamia and Egypt. In any case they always saw him directing his activity towards themselves, revealing his essential nature as just and merciful under the terms of the covenant – first in the Law of Moses, and then as described by Jeremiah – writing his laws in their hearts (Jer.31:31).

The Old Testament is a story of the discovery of God by a people and of a people by God – a people chosen by himself. It is the story of their refinement, as silver is refined in a fire. This reveals his nature to those who will remain loyal enough to discover it. Some fall by the wayside in Sinai, longing for the fleshpots of Egypt. Some fall prey to the worship of the baals in Canaan. Some succumb to the easy living in Babylon. Some are bewitched by the influence of Hellenism. Some undergo a kind of *rigor-mortis* in strict obedience to the Law. Some lose their conscience in reliance upon the fact that their salvation is assured because they "have Abraham as (their) father." The faithful remnant shrinks until it is embodied in one man, Jesus, who is the Christ. Here in this climactic event the fullness of God is revealed to men in the life of one man. Yahweh empties himself of all the power and glory of the Genesis Creator, and Law Giver, the Exodus God of history, the Judges God of War, the Kings God of government. He reappears in the life of the lowliest, most typical of all men: one born in a stable in an obscure corner of the world, a carpenter by trade. A man in whom the fullness of God was pleased to dwell. A man whose life was one of perfect obedience, a perfect example of maturity, and example of God's plan for every man who will allow himself to be possessed of the will of God. The Old Testament, the Old Covenant, the Old Agreement is fulfilled, and the new has come. The 12 tribes become the 12 apostles, the Servant Israel becomes the Servant Jesus, and another era emerges and the voice of God is heard again – "Behold, I make all things new."

[1]Cf. Zech. 13:4ff., "On that day every prophet will be ashamed of his vision when he prophesies; he will not put on a hairy mantle to deceive, but he will say, 'I am no prophet . . . . ' "

SUGGESTED BIBLICAL READINGS

CHAPTER 3	Genesis 1:1 - 2:24
CHAPTER 4	Genesis 3
CHAPTER 5	Genesis 4 - 9; 11:1-9
CHAPTER 6	Genesis 12 Genesis 13 Genesis 17 Genesis 19 Genesis 20:1-18 Genesis 22 Genesis 24 Genesis 25:21-34 Genesis 27 Genesis 27:10-22 Genesis 29 Genesis 31 Genesis 37 Genesis 39 - 41 Genesis 47 Genesis 50
CHAPTER 7	Exodus 1:1 - 6:1 Exodus 11:4-10 Exodus 12:1-13, 21-50 Exodus 13 - 15 Exodus 18 Exodus 19 Exodus 20:1-17 Exodus 20:22 - 23:33
CHAPTER 8	Joshua 1 Joshua 2 Joshua 6 Joshua 24 Judges 4 Judges 5
CHAPTER 9	Judges 6 Judges 7 Judges 8 Judges 11 Judges 12
CHAPTER 10	Judges 13:24 - 16:31 Judges 17 Judges 18

CHAPTER 11

I Samuel 4:1b-7, 9, 10a, 11-14
16-21a, 22
I Samuel 5:1-4, 6-12
I Samuel 6
I Samuel 7:1
I Samuel 9:1-8, 10-14, 16-21a, 22
I Samuel 10:1-6, 11-16a
I Samuel 11:1-11, 15
I Samuel 13:2-5ac, 6, 7a, 15b-17,
23
I Samuel 14:1, 2, 3b-46, 52
I Samuel 16:14-23
I Samuel 18:6b-8a, 9, 20, 22-29
I Samuel 19:11-17
I Samuel 20:4-10, 12-17, 24-34
I Samuel 21:1-9
I Samuel 22:1-4, 6-18, 20-23
I Samuel 23:1-11ac, 12-14a
I Samuel 27:1-3a, 4-6a, 8a, 9,
10, 12
I Samuel 29:1-4, 6-24, 26

II Samuel 1
II Samuel 2:1-9
II Samuel 3:1, 6-29
II Samuel 4:1-12
II Samuel 5:3-5
II Samuel 21:15-22
II Samuel 6:2-12
II Samuel 8:14b-18
II Samuel 9
II Samuel 10:1-14

CHAPTER 12

II Samuel 11:1-27
II Samuel 12:15b-31
II Samuel 14:25-33
II Samuel 15:1-37
II Samuel 16:1-23
II Samuel 17:1-29
II Samuel 18:1-33

I Kings 1
I Kings 2:10-12
I Kings 3 - 5
I Kings 7:1-14
I Kings 10
I Kings 11

CHAPTER 13

I Kings 12
I Kings 16:21-34
I Kings 17 - 19
I Kings 21
I Kings 22:40

II Kings 2
II Kings 5
II Kings 21:1-9, 16-18
II Kings 22
II Kings 23:1-3
II Kings 24
II Kings 25

CHAPTER 14

Exodus 28:41
Exodus 29:7, 29, 36
Exodus 30:30

Judges 9:8

I Samuel 16:3-12

I Kings 1:34-39
I Kings 19:16

Job 26:12-13

Psalms 2
Psalms 48:2-4

Isaish 25:6
Isaiah 27:1
Isaiah 30:7
Isaiah 40:1-3
Isaiah 61:1

Jeremiah 23:5, 6
Jeremiah 26:1, 2
Jeremiah 27:1
Jeremiah 28:1
Jeremiah 33:15, 16

Ezekiel 34:22-25
Ezekiel 37:24

Amos 9:3

CHAPTER 15

II Kings 18:1-8

Jeremiah 1 - 8
Jeremiah 36

CHAPTER 17

Hosea

CHAPTER 18

Isaiah 1
Isaiah 2:6 - 4:1
Isaiah 5
Isaiah 6
Isaiah 7:1-16
Isaiah 8:1-18
Isaiah 9:8-10:4a
Isaiah 10:5-15a, 28-32

Isaiah 14:24-32
Isaiah 17:1-3a
Isaiah 18:1-6
Isaiah 20:1-6
Isaiah 22:1-14, 15-25
Isaiah 28:7-22
Isaiah 29:1-4, 9, 10, 13-15
Isaiah 30:1-5, 8-19
Isaiah 31:1-3

CHAPTER 19

Deuteronomy 12 - 26
II Chronicles 34

CHAPTER 20

Jeremiah 1:1-10
Jeremiah 5
Jeremiah 7
Jeremiah 11:18-23
Jeremiah 12:1-6
Jeremiah 15:10-18
Jeremiah 17:14-18
Jeremiah 18:18-23
Jeremiah 19
Jeremiah 20:1-12, 14-18
Jeremiah 26
Jeremiah 32
Jeremiah 36

Ezekiel 1
Ezekiel 2:1-7
Ezekiel 4:1-8
Ezekiel 5
Ezekiel 11:14-20
Ezekiel 16:1-5
Ezekiel 18:1-4
Ezekiel 25:1-5
Ezekiel 26:1-6
Ezekiel 34
Ezekiel 37

II Isaiah 40:1-11
II Isaiah 42:1-4
II Isaiah 49:1-6
II Isaiah 50:4-11
II Isaiah 52:13-53:12

CHAPTER 21

Job 1
Job 2
Job 3
Job 4
Job 5
Job 6
Job 38
Job 42

Proverbs 1:1-7
Proverbs 3:1-20
Proverbs 6:6-8
Proverbs 15:1,2
Proverbs 16:1-3, 18-33
Proverbs 33:18, 19

Jonah

Ecclesiastes 1:1-11
Ecclesiastes 2
Ecclesiastes 3:1-9
Ecclesiastes 12

CHAPTER 22

Daniel 7 - 12

Joel

Ezekiel 38
Ezekiel 39